What Others Are Saying About One Way Ticket To Kansas

Ozzie Tinman explains how his wife, with Borderline Personality Disorder took over his life, and how he claimed it back; not by trying to fix his wife, but by taking responsibility for his own issues. Readers who have had a partner with BPD will find this friendly, empathetic book helpful in learning how they too can stop Walking on Eggshells and take charge of their own life.

> Randy Kreger
> Stop Walking on Eggshells

I often run into family members at their wits end as they share their tearful stories. My recommendation to their relief is On Way Ticket To Kansas.

> Kathi Stringer, PHD
> Expert Group Facilitator

Your Book has opened my eyes as to how it feels to be involved in a relationship with a person suffering from Borderline Personality Disorder. Having the illness myself, it is a book that I am sending to all my loved ones.

> Kymberly
> BPD Sufferer and
> Support Group Member

One Way Ticket To Kansas is a book that is greatly needed to help those that are suffering from the abuse as a result of being in a relationship with someone with Borderline Personality Disorder. During my 8 years as an MFT, I have seen the destructive effects of this disorder on the friends and families of someone diagnosed, and search for resources to help them cope. It is obvious that One Way Ticket To Kansas was written from the heart and something that Ozzie Tinman lived through, and overcame. His journey will assist many others in their own personal journey and struggles in coping.

Judy Speak, MFT

This book is a must for anyone struggling to come to terms with the mess they've found themselves in when they realize they are living with someone who has Borderline Personality Disorder. How did I get here? Who is this person? Why didn't I know before it was too late? What do I do now? How can I be sure it's them and not me? All these questions and more are thoroughly dealt with in this excellent book, One Way Ticket To Kansas.

This book puts it all into perspective and helps you reclaim your life in ways you never expected, but are not difficult to achieve.

Ron Berglas
Support Group Member

One Way Ticket To Kansas

**Caring About Someone With
Borderline Personality Disorder
And Finding A Healthy You**

Written By: Ozzie Tinman

**Bebes & Gregory Publications
Murrieta, Ca**

Bebes & Gregory Publications
39657 Bayonne Pl, Murrieta, Ca 92562

ISBN: 978-0-9767873-8-9

Library of Congress Control: 2005922464

*This book is dedicated to my mother.
Without your love, support, and
understanding, I would not have had the
courage to face the uphill struggles that led
to my personal growth throughout this
experience. I love you.*

Your Hito

Notice

This book documents the personal experiences and perspective of the author.

The author is not a psychologist, psychiatrist, counselor, or therapist.

While this book may contribute to your understanding of your situation and of Borderline Personality Disorder, it is not a substitute for professional treatment. If you are in distress, please seek assistance from a trained and licensed professional.

If you are in an abusive situation and in danger of physical harm, please seek a safe shelter. Many US locations have domestic violence outreach listed online. Please do not hesitate to seek assistance if your well being is in jeopardy.

If you have thoughts of ending your life, immediately call your therapist, counselor, doctor, or emergency assistance. These people are trained to help you in such a crisis.

Contents

Acknowledgements 9

Introduction 11

1. One Way Ticket To Kansas 16

2. What Is Borderline Personality Disorder? 26

3. The Ozzie Tinman Story 48

4. An Honest Look At Yourself 66

5. Taking Care Of Number 1 90

6. BPD Defense Mechanisms and Control Tactics 110

7. Ozzie Stink' Thinkin' 134

8. Leaving Oz Is A State Of Mind 154

Afterwards: Ozzie Tinman 20 Years Later 160

Appendix: Ozzie Dictionary 172

Acknowledgements

During the course of writing this book, I received the assistance and support of many people whose impact on my life is immeasurable. I would like to acknowledge these people:

For your love, guidance and advice, which has helped me get through this most difficult trials of my life, I would like to thank my mother JoAnn, father Bob, step-father Russ, grandparents Ruben and Martha, aunt Sophie, aunt Melissa, and brother John. I would also like to give a heartfelt thank you to Chelsie, who showed me what true unconditional love is by providing support and love, during a time when she, herself, was having to adjust to major changes in her life. I am both, proud and admire you, for the strong person you have become. Next, I would like to thank Ashley for your constant reminders that even in the toughest of times, a smile can help you get through the day. You are beautiful, and strong, and I am lucky to have you as a cousin. Last, but not least, I would like to acknowledge my aunt Rose. She was the embodiment of love, happiness, and selflessness. Although she has passed, her love and devotion to family and friends lives on.

For your wisdom and clinical assistance, I would like to thank Elyce Benham from the Land of Oz online support groups. Your devotion to helping those diagnosed with BPD, and their families, cannot be acknowledged enough. You have touched so many lives, and asked for nothing in return other than for those helped to pay-it-forward. I would also like to thank Rosalie Chaffee, MFT. Your insightful questions and validation of my experiences led to my writing of this book. It was while I was sharing with you that I discovered that many of the answers were right in front of me.

For reminding me to be compassionate and to seek further understanding of the pain a person with BPD suffers, I must thank Kymberly. As a BPD sufferer, and someone I am proud to have called a friend, you have provided me invaluable insight into this condition, and the underlying fears that lead to many of the volatile behaviors.

Ozzie Tinman

Introduction

Borderline Personality Disorder (BPD) is a crippling disorder, not only for the person that is diagnosed, but for the family and friends that care for the person as well. The pain that this disorder brings stretches far and wide, consuming and creating absolute chaos for everything and everyone in its path. Parents, spouses, children, and friends are all thrown in a whirlwind of destruction, feeling alone to wonder if there is anything that they can do. Where do they start? Where does it end? Is there any hope?

The symptoms of BPD have been noted as far back as the 1940's, but has only recently been given an actual diagnosis criteria in the DSM-IV in 1980. It is a relatively new diagnosis in which researchers are struggling feverishly to try to address. However, very little is known about the disorder and its treatment. What is known is that it wreaks havoc in the lives of those that are exposed to it, and that there is no current uniformed treatment for it.

In the absence of complete research studies, and the little information that is actually known about treating this disorder, there is even less information known to assist those which are affected through the connection of family and friendship ties. This is the purpose of this book.

After being told of our significant other's diagnosis, many of us ran to the bookstore, or library, expecting to find a collection of titles that could explain in layman's terms what Borderline Personality Disorder is, and how it affects us as the people that care about the diagnosed person. However, when we checked the shelves, all we found were clinical books that require a doctorate degree to interpret, or books that focused on the experience of the diagnosed person. We also found that many of the books written for people diagnosed with BPD were very general and did not present the hard facts of this disorder. They seemed to pull a lot of punches when it came to explaining the severity of the behaviors that we were experiencing in our relationships.

What is the reason for this? Quite simply, the books that are written for people diagnosed with BPD traditionally present the information in a very soft manner so the diagnosed person will continue to read the book. Confronting this population with the severity of their behavior, and the impact it has on others, would likely result in the person refusing to continue reading the book, as their lack of coping mechanisms may push them away from seeking information regarding the true ugliness of this disorder and their accountability.

As those that are being so seriously affected by the person with this disorder and having the desire to understand it, we want true, honest answers about what is happening in our lives. We want no punches pulled. We want information given to us in a straight-forward manner. However, upon walking into the bookstore or library, we discovered that there are few books, other than Stop Walking on Eggshells, that addresses the needs of the person who cares about the diagnosed. There is little guidance for those of us that want to learn about BPD, and how we can address the issues within ourselves that allow the destructive traits of our loved one to affect us so greatly.

I am not a formally trained professional in Borderline Personality Disorder. I do hold a degree in Psychology; however, I am not a trained therapist or counselor with a formal education focused on BPD treatment. Rather, I am a regular person just like you. I learned about BPD, its destructive effects, means of coping, and means of healing through the life experience of being married, for nine years, to a woman diagnosed with BPD. Throughout this time, I did enough research, participated in many support groups, and educated myself through the internet, read books, talking to experts in BPD, and dealing with my wife's destructive behaviors, that I have developed a wealth of information about this disorder. I wrote this book to share this information in a way that you deserve; in layman's terms with honesty, truthfulness, and without pulling punches. I hope you benefit from the information in this book as much as I benefited from gathering it. I wish you

Godspeed on your journey of trying to make sense of the crossroads that you have found yourself at and the difficult choices that lay ahead.

Chapter 1

One Way Ticket To Kansas

Chapter 1

One Way Ticket To Kansas

I would like to welcome you to the beginning of your journey to Kansas. Why Kansas? If you are familiar with the communities and support available for people who care about someone with Borderline Personality Disorder (BPD), you are well aware of the metaphors of the Frank Baum book, The Wizard of Oz, and how the world you find yourself in parallels that of Oz in many aspects. If you are new to the world of BPD then find yourself a comfortable place, a decent light, and take notes. The metaphor of Oz is one that you must be familiar with as a means of communicating with other Ozzies.

What is an Ozzie? An Ozzie is you and me. A person who cares for someone with BPD that has visited, remains in, tried to escape, or has successfully escaped the warped and delusional world of a person diagnosed with BPD. Depending on the community and support group that you connect with, Ozzies are also referred to as Nons, Non BPDs, BPSO's (Borderline Personality's Significant Other), or Kansans (for those that have escaped). For simplicity sake of this book, I will use Ozzie in reference to a person that is married to, lives with, or cares for someone diagnosed with, or suspected to have, BPD.

The metaphors of Oz are very significant on the journey an Ozzie ventures on as he or she grows and learns about themselves. Escaping Oz is not only about learning to cope, adapt, or escape the control of the person with BPD, but also requires that you face many facts about yourself that drew you (and probably continues to) to their specific traits. Many Ozzies find the strength to leave their troubled relationship, only to find themselves back in a similar relationship with another person with BPD (or difficult personality traits). These Ozzies remain in Oz simply because they did not look within themselves for the true root, and tried to blame the outcome solely on their partner's disorder. Plain and simple; we landed in Oz by choice, and until you focus on yourself you will remain there.

Ok, now that we have that said, we can define the various metaphors of this land that we call Oz.

Kansas: Reality. It is the place where most healthy people live and can relate on an emotional and physical level. It is reality based in today's world. It is rational and makes sense.

Oz: The "reality" of the person with Borderline Personality Disorder. It is the place that you, as the Ozzie, have been sucked into and succumb to be part of. It is a place where distortions live, where emotions define what reality is, and those emotions and reality are ever changing. To a person with BPD, Oz makes sense because they define the rules of logic and rationale, and their perceptions of what "reality" will serve the purpose of justifying their unacceptable behaviors. To an Ozzie, it is a constant source of frustration, pain, and anguish in which things rarely make sense.

Tornado: The tornado represents the whirlwind of emotions and anger the person with BPD displays. It is what picked you up and dropped you off in Oz. It is a state of confusion, constant chaos, and crazy-making behavior displayed by the person with BPD.

During your trip through Oz you will play many roles. There is Dorothy, the Lion, the Scarecrow, and the Tin Man. Which role you play will depend upon your situation.

Dorothy: Confused, searching for home, and trying to make sense of the "reality" that she finds herself in. She finds herself where the rules of her reality are no longer consistent, and that another person's ever-changing perceptions dictate what "reality" is at any given moment. She goes on a difficult journey to the Emerald City, simply to find out that the answers were right under her nose (on her feet) the entire time.

Lion: Looking for some courage. An Ozzie will need to face many obstacles on their journey back to Kansas. If you remain with the person diagnosed with BPD, you need the courage to set solid boundaries and insist that you are respected and not abused. You may need the courage to leave the abusive relationship, or seek answers about yourself as to why you landed in Oz in the first place. You will find yourself as the Lion many times on this journey. Like the Lion, you must find the courage to confront the challenges both, before you and within yourself.

Scarecrow: The Scarecrow was searching for a brain. In our case, we must go on a journey to define what is real and what is an illusion. How does our brain interpret things? Perhaps the way we want to see them rather than how they truly are? This will be a question that you must answer. You are going to have to come to realization that your perceptions of reality are skewed. You will need to re-learn what is real, and use logic and rationale to not get sucked back into Oz. What is real, and what is illusion, in our world is not always simple, nor easy to discover. The Scarecrow also represents the research and knowledge you are going to have to seek in order to escape Oz. The foundation of our survival truly is education and we will need to use our brain to remind us to stay tethered to reality. Research BPD, find answers, and remain in reality.

Tin Man: One of the first steps you are going to have to take is to find your heart...for yourself. You are going to have to learn to love yourself enough to take care of yourself. This is not an easy task considering you have likely invested years in completely neglecting yourself to care for every whim of the person with BPD. You've been groomed and taught that peace and happiness only exists when the person with BPD is being completely catered to, and their contentment serves as the center of the universe. You begin to believe that you only get to experience acceptance/love by being completely selfless and giving, and that your needs matter very little in the grand scheme of your relationship. The Tin Man wanted love. He sang of finding it and its effects, when all along, all he had to do was find love for himself. Loving yourself allows you to love others.

Poppy Fields: As the opium from the poppy flowers are used as a drug to numb a person, so does this disorder serve to numb your entire life. There are times when you walk around like a zombie, wondering if you are truly real. Where are you, where are you going, you're not quite sure. Do you even exist? Do you even matter? This is the feeling of you losing yourself and your emotions, as you devote your every second to the person with BPD. The person with BPD relies upon you being in this altered state of haziness and detachment, as it makes you more susceptible to their manipulations and control tactics.

Emerald City: This is the perceived end of your journey. This is where you believe you need to go for all your answers. This is where the great Wizard lives that will bestow upon you everything you could ever ask for. But does it really exist? In your version of Oz, is it the end of your trip where Kansas is a hop-skip-and a jump away? Or is it an elaborate ploy meant to deceive, and when you arrive you find out that all along you had the power to control your own destiny? The metaphor of the Emerald City is very unique, as it is a metaphor that every Ozzie seems to have their own definition. Personally, I saw it as a mirage. The center point where illusion ruled. It was the place where the Wizard lived, the greatest illusionist of them all. It was where we found out that the Wizard was nothing more than a carnival magician, that did not possess any true powers. Like a person with BPD, he controlled the reality of those around him, thus giving him the power to control the people that trusted him.

Apple Trees: Indicative of the harsh responses of the person with BPD; only in Oz would you get slapped and attacked for picking an apple. Ozzies experience similar responses in their relationship we share with the person with BPD. Only in our world can we be yelled at and persecuted for making a sandwich, going to bed late, or simply coming home from work. There seems to be negative consequences attached to simple everyday behaviors that the person with BPD takes personally. The illogical responses and punishments become commonplace, and the Ozzie begins to alter their behavior in an attempt to avoid the negative consequences, rather than addressing the irrational demands of the person with BPD.

Horse of a Different Color: When Dorothy and her friends first enter the Emerald City they were met by a carriage drawn by a horse that changed colors every time they looked at it. This is the world of an Ozzie: constantly changing, confusing, and lacking definition. The rules change at a seconds notice and you never quite understand what to expect from moment to moment. Just when you think something is green, you find out it is blue. Today's world is different than yesterday's, and you can anticipate it changing tomorrow as well.

The Wizard: The person diagnosed with Borderline Personality Disorder. The Wizard is the master of illusion. He convinced an entire world that he was all-powerful, capable of bestowing great gifts and magical wonder. However, when he was unmasked, he was shown to be a mediocre circus illusionist that possessed no true powers other than the ability to deceive people. The person with BPD lives life in a similar manner. They initially appear to be wonderful, capable of giving, and magical. Yet when they are unmasked, they are found to be an illusion, an image larger than life, that's created by manipulating those around them to serve their own means.

Through your journey you will find many more metaphors by reading the book or watching the movie Wizard of Oz. There seems to be an endless supply of them, and all have substantial meaning to each Ozzie. I have given you the staple metaphors that most Ozzies agree upon the meaning. However, part of your great journey will be to think for yourself and discover what is truly meaningful and important to you.

So welcome to Air Kansas. Please fasten your seat belts, face forward (and refuse to look back into Oz), as we begin our departure towards Kansas. My name is Ozzie Tinman and I will be your Captain.

Chapter 2

What is
Borderline Personality Disorder?

Chapter 2

What Is Borderline Personality Disorder?

In order to explain what BPD is, you must first understand what a Personality Disorder is and how it is different from other forms of mental illnesses. A Personality Disorder is an enduring pattern of behavior that deviates considerably from the expectations of an individual culture. The pattern of behavior is pervasive, unlikely to change, is stable over time, and leads to distress and impairment in interpersonal relationships. To be classified as a personality disorder, the person's behavior must be so pervasive that it causes distress, both for the individual with the disorder, as well as those that interact with him or her.

A personality disorder differs from many other mental illnesses in that it can't simply be treated through medication management to address brain chemical imbalances. Many Ozzies wish it were that easy. However, the behaviors and traits that define a personality disorder are just that, engrained in the person's personality. Some of these behaviors have been learned by the person at a very young age and used for protection against being hurt, otherwise known as a defense mechanism. Some people develop the traits due to their genetic predisposition. Some personality disorders develop due to a combination of genetic predisposition and environmental influences (lack of nurturing, abuse, etc.). So in order for the person with the personality disorder to change their behavior they must: 1) admit that their way of thinking and interpreting the world has been faulty for a great portion of their life, and 2) be willing to change these destructive behaviors and accept new behaviors in their place. To address personality disorders, the person must be willing to learn to be a new person. As you can imagine, very few people diagnosed with a personality disorder are willing to take these first steps of admitting that their perception of the world is abnormal. And can you really blame them? What would your response be if someone walked up to you and told you that your entire perception of reality is just a manifestation of your mind? That what you think is real, actually does not exist, and your entire life is a complete illusion created to protect you from an unknown perceived danger. Would you be willing to dismiss all you have ever known as reality? Or would you fight to your last breath to prove that you are not crazy and your world does make sense? This is what your loved one diagnosed with BPD finds themselves facing.

Now that you know what a personality disorder is and why it is so difficult to treat, we are ready to go onto what traits are required for a diagnosis of Borderline Personality Disorder. Per the DSM-IV, in total there are nine traits associated with this disorder. For a person to be diagnosed with BPD,

they must display at least five of these nine
personality traits. They are as follows:

1) Frantic efforts to avoid real or imagined
   abandonment. Note: Do not include suicide
   or self-mutilating behavior covered in (5).
2) A pattern of unstable and intense
   interpersonal relationships characterized by
   alternating between extremes of idolization
   and devaluation.
3) Identity disturbance: markedly and
   persistently unstable self-image or no sense
   of self.
4) Impulsivity in at least two areas that are
   potentially self-damaging (e.g., spending,
   sex, substance abuse, shoplifting, reckless
   driving, binge eating). Note: Do not include
   suicidal or self-mutilating behavior covered
   in (5).
5) Recent suicidal behavior, gestures, or
   threats, or self-mutilating behavior.
6) Affective instability due to marked
   reactivity of mood (e.g., intense episodic
   dysphoria, irritability, or anxiety usually
   lasting a few hours and only rarely more
   than a few days. [Dysphoria is the opposite
   of euphoria. It is a mixture of depression,
   anxiety, rage, and despair.]
7) Chronic feelings of emptiness.

8) Inappropriate, intense anger or difficulty controlling anger (e.g., frequent displays of temper, constant anger, recurrent physical fights.)
9) Transient, stress related paranoid ideations or severe dissociative symptoms.

So what does all this mean in layman's terms? Let's go through them one by one.

1) Frantic efforts to avoid real or imagined abandonment. Note: Do not include suicidal or self-mutilating behavior covered in (5).

Driving much of the person with BPD's fears is the belief that they do not deserve to be loved or cared for. They believe that all the people they care about will abandon them and leave them helpless to face this world alone. As a result, they engage in frantic behaviors to keep those that they care about from leaving them. Unfortunately, many of these behaviors are destructive to the relationship, and in turn the frantic efforts to hold onto the person are the exact behaviors that drive that person far away. Some of the destructive behaviors to maintain possession of the loved one are blackmail, threats, learned helplessness, and distortion campaigns. Many times the person with BPD will make it so difficult for the Ozzie to leave that they will stay in the relationship out of fear of losing friends, family, their reputation, employment and to avoid threats of criminal accusations. When the person with BPD is in fear of being abandoned, all bets are off. They will do almost anything to avoid being left.

In addition to frantic attempts to hold onto their loved one, the person with BPD may also intentionally drive people they care away. Why you may ask. Simply to beat the person to the punch, and avoid the hurt of being abandoned. The person with BPD is already convinced that you are leaving. So rather than opening themselves up to the pain of being left, they will intentionally make staying with them so painful that the Ozzie has no choice but to leave. In doing this, the person with BPD has just validated their belief that everyone abandons them, and they were able to control when the Ozzie does leave. This helps ease the impact of being abandoned.

2) A pattern of unstable and intense interpersonal relationships characterized by alternating between extremes of idolization and devaluation.

You are her knight in shining armor, her savior, and the man of her dreams. You are everything she ever wanted. She brags about you to friends and family, saying you are the perfect husband, the most wonderful father, you are the light of her life. You walk around proud that your partner loves you so much and that she has placed you on a pedestal for the world to see. Then one day she looks at you with disgust in her eyes, accuses you of having affairs, you are a controlling father, and terrible lover. No matter how hard you try, you can't do anything right. Guess what my friend...you have just been "Split."

Splitting is the process in which a person diagnosed with BPD alternates between adoring and loathing the person that they are emotionally close to. The BPD sees the world in terms of black and white, good and evil, completely right and completely wrong. So when you are in their favor, you are raised to the level where they worship and adore you. But one false step and you are seen as Satan himself. There is no middle ground, no gray area. You are either split "White" (all good) or "Black" (all bad). If you live with someone diagnosed with BPD get used to it. It is how they make sense of the world. There is nothing you can do about it. Splitting can happen for any reason, and it rarely make sense to the Ozzie. This is where the metaphor of the Apple Tree comes in. In Kansas you can pick an apple, eat it and enjoy it. However, in Oz, simply picking an apple without permission could result in harsh consequences and being called a vile creature for doing something so terrible.

The interpretation of the world in black and white terms wreaks havoc on a relationship. Much of life and reality lies in the gray area of rights and wrongs. However, when dealing with someone who sees only black and white, the requirements of absolute perfection and complete literal statements becomes an impossible task. Any act by you that is seen as less than perfect could result in the splitting of you to black.

After a while the worry of wondering whether you will be good or evil in the eyes of your significant other, is enough to cause physical ailments such as stomach knots, ulcers, heart conditions, and other conditions associated with stress. You are constantly walking on your tip toes to avoid what consequences are around every corner.

Splitting is a byproduct of the core issue, within the person diagnosed with BPD, that they are both: terrified of being alone, as well as being so intimately close with someone that they expose their faults and their own imperfections. As a result they get into a tug-of-war with their emotions, which is ultimately taken out on and given to the Ozzie to carry for them (projection). What happens is the person with BPD will draw you in with kindness and give you signals that they want you near them. They want to insure for themselves that you will not abandon them so they strive to create a situation in which you do not want to or can't leave. However, there will come a time when you are drawn too close. You will get so close to the person with BPD that their faults will become apparent, and their panic response will be triggered. In a nutshell, their brain will scream, "danger, danger, intruder. This person is going to see that I am broken!!!" As a result they will violently push you away. They will push you far enough away that you lose intimacy and connectedness. Just when you start to lose hope and start to make arrangements to leave, they will start the drawing in process again. Ozzies call this "hoovering", named after the strong suction of a Hoover vacuum. And here lies the unstable and intense interpersonal relationship.

3) Identity disturbance: markedly and persistently unstable self-image or no sense of self.

All of us are familiar with the old amnesia cliché, "Who am I? What am I? Where am I?" It usually draws a few laughs and giggles when done in a social setting and used as humor. However, when you are a person with BPD, these questions are not a laughing matter. They are how you live, every day, every minute of your life.

Many people diagnosed with this disorder had some serious disruption in their personality and identity development. Whether this disruption was caused by physical abuse, sexual abuse, an overwhelmingly controlling caretaker, etc. is not the responsibility for us Ozzies to solve; however, we do need to be aware that the person with BPD has absolutely no idea who they truly are, or what their purpose in life is. They go through their day with a feeling of emptiness, as though they are missing the one puzzle piece that will explain their true purpose. The problem is that they search feverishly for this missing piece, try on many hats, and start many adventures, only to discover that they are every bit as empty after their achievement as they were before they started. They take on huge tasks only to quit right before they finish. Or if they do finish and achieve, they belittle their accomplishments. My wife trained for a year and ran the LA Marathon, a notable achievement in anyone's brag book. However, after she finished the race she could only focus on how her time was not good enough and the 26-mile run was a disappointment.

The person with BPD's search for an identity is never ending. They may go to college, but have no sense of direction as to where they want that education to take them. They may surround themselves with people they admire, attempt to adopt their traits, and emulate their behaviors. They may start and stop many careers only to find out that none are fulfilling for them. They may choose to be a stay at home parent, only to later complain that they would have been happier having paying employment.

In my wife's case she went through college, achieved multiple advances degrees, and secured what many would have considered an ideal job for a woman with young children, where she only had to work while our children were in school. About two years into her employment she decided that her life was not fulfilling, and that true happiness was in being a full-time housewife and mother. I made enough money to support her wishes to not work, so she quit her job. Shortly after quitting, she decided staying home left her feeling "empty" and without a purpose, and she wanted to start working again, but in a different field. I did not realize it then, but what my wife was doing was searching for an identity that made her feel complete. As with many people with BPD, this search is never ending because their missing piece does not exist. The emptiness is in the very fabric of their being. Nothing that the person with BPD will ever do or accomplish will be good enough for them.

4) Impulsivity in at least two areas that are potentially self-damaging (e.g., spending, sex, substance abuse, shoplifting, reckless driving, binge eating). Note: Do not include suicidal or self-mutilating behavior covered in (5).

Many people with BPD display behaviors that indicate poor self-control and spontaneous recklessness. This can include gambling, drug use, sexual promiscuity, thrill-seeking behaviors, stealing, eating disorders, etc. The way in which the person with BPD engages in this behavior is similar to a drug addict needing their drug of choice. The focus is on the current need for the destructive behavior, and to satisfy the urge to engage in it. The person with BPD rarely sees the long-term consequences of their behavior, as their primary focus is on the moment at hand. In reviewing your finances you may find out that your partner is spending extraordinary amounts of money and having little to show for it. You may discover that your loved one is involved with many sexual partners or that they have a history of drug use. Many Ozzies have been shocked to discover that their partner, whom for a long time displayed a June Cleaver image, had been concealing many skeletons in their closet, and are engaged in many destructive behaviors that exposes themselves, as well as their family, to huge risks.

In my marriage, it was common for our family to make ends meet financially by a couple of hundred dollars per month. I always trusted my wife to spend responsibly and to take care of the financial interests of our family by not engaging in a lot of frivolous spending. Unfortunately, I never checked her spending. So I accepted that essentially being a one-income household, we were making ends meet to the best of our capabilities. However, after 9 years of marriage, I made the hard decision to leave my wife. In doing so, I took the bills with me and told her I would pay all our financial obligations with my income. Further, she could keep her check from her part-time employment and spend it as she saw fit. As I walked out the door she told me that we could never afford to live separately.

In reviewing our financial records, what did I find? You guessed it. So much frivolous spending that we actually had in excess of $1,500-$2,500 per month going to absolutely nothing of value.

Through budgeting the large amounts of money that she was spending, that I was not aware of (my own fault), I was able to secure myself in my own apartment, pay all my extra costs, pay down our accrued financial obligations, and still have excess for discretionary spending. My point is, for years I assumed that my wife was being responsible and dependable with our finances. I later found out that she did have spending issues that placed our family in a position what could have been disastrous had we encountered an emergency that required us to produce cash quickly. Fortunately, that did not happen.

Although spending was one of my wife's subjects of lack of self-control, many Ozzies have discovered that their spouse was engaged in many extramarital affairs. I have also spoken to many Ozzies that have come home to be told by their partners that they must move out of their homes because the person with BPD lost the title due to gambling debt. I have heard of many instances of closet drug use. Abusing controlled substances is very common among people with BPD. A safe approach to dealing with someone with BPD, and self-control issues, is to assume that they have a skeleton or two in the closet. Watch your money and know where it is going. Watch for the person with BPD staying out late at night or indications of affairs. It may be painful for you to face the hard truth that your loved one is engaged in harmful behaviors; however, learning the hard truth may be much easier than paying the huge consequences of not knowing.

5) Recent suicidal behaviors, gestures, or threats, or self-mutilating behavior.

The description of the trait speaks for itself. A person diagnosed with BPD may become suicidal at times. This can result from them splitting themselves black and losing all hope that they could ever be of any good. Keep in mind that they continually struggle with black and white thinking and live for the moment, not the long term. When they come to a situation where they can not avoid responsibility and must accept that they have done something that they view as "bad" they will swing to an extreme, and thus believe they are a horrible person. They feel empty, useless, and hopeless, and like nothing they do is "good." They are evil. Their self-worth and confidence is nonexistent. At the time of splitting themselves, they truly believe that there is no reason for them to go on living.

A person with BPD may also display self-mutilating behavior. This can result for a couple of different reasons. First it can be a form of self-punishment as a result of splitting. Perhaps the person with BPD does feel that they are damaged, no good, empty, etc, but actual suicide is not an extreme they are willing to go to. The person with BPD may cut themselves, slam their hand in a door, or hit their head, as a form of punishment. Another reason they may self-mutilate is simply to "feel." As they struggle with feeling empty, feelings unreal, numbness to their world, and feelings of total loss of control; cutting or injuring themselves can bring back a sense of realism to them. Feeling the pain and sensation of the cut may allow them to feel as though they truly exist. If they feel it, then it is real. They are real.

As an Ozzie you need to recognize when the person with BPD is in the process of splitting themselves and when they are most prone to these behaviors. If you see depression within them begin to arise, recognize that the person is very down on themselves, or that they express self-harming ideas, contact their therapist immediately. Don't be afraid to tell the therapist when you believe your loved one is a danger to themselves. A therapist is trained to handle such a situation. You are not.

As an Ozzie you must remind yourself that you do not have the power to stop another's suicidal thoughts and/or attempts. They must take responsibility for their own thoughts and actions. Sometimes the person will express to you that they are going to kill themselves. A common response from an Ozzie will be to try to convince the person with BPD not to do it. The Ozzie will beg and try to talk sense into their loved one. They will try to "fix" the situation by attempting to display that they care to an extreme. In reality, all the Ozzie did was transfer a whole lot of control and power to the person with BPD to use suicide as a manipulation against them in the future. Many times the best response to a person with BPD threatening suicide is to simply say, "I do not want you to harm yourself, but I can not stop you. It is a decision that you are going to have to make." Refuse to take responsibility for their actions and place them firmly back where they belong, with the person making the threats.

6) Affective instability due to marked reactivity of mood (e.g., intense episodic dysphoria, irritability, or anxiety usually lasting a few hours and only rarely more than a few days). [Dysphoria is the opposite of euphoria. It is a mixture of depression, anxiety, rage, and despair.]

One of the consistent indicators of BPD is a rapid cycle of mood swings. A person with BPD could literally go from raging anger towards you to wanting to have passionate sex with you within a matter of minutes. Then after lovemaking, they swing into depression. Within a couple of hours they could have multiple swings of extreme powerful emotions, all of which are very confusing to the Ozzie because the mood swings have very little to do with what is happening in the present circumstances. Rather, as someone with BPD goes throughout their day, their emotional responses are triggered by subconscious cues that we, as Ozzies, may not be aware of.

An example could be lovemaking. What if your partner has unresolved sexual issues that they are repressing and blocking out? You have what you consider to be a close, intimate, and sharing sexual experience. During lovemaking your partner seems very passionate and seems to enjoy the experience as much as yourself. After finishing you look at your partner and give her a loving kiss, only to find out that she is laying next to you crying. You ask why, and she can't give you an answer. Your partner, within an instant, has swung from passionate, into depression. The closeness, intimacy, and sexual experience served as a trigger for a mood swing; however, neither of you understand why.

The person with BPD goes throughout their day experiencing these mood swings. Triggers happen throughout the day, touching a nerve, that causes their emotional responses to bounce back and forth. The mood swings are unpredictable, and for the most part the origin of the swings are not understood.

To remedy the unknown trigger or cause of the mood swing, the person with BPD will manufacture a cause. In the above example, where the Ozzie discovers their partner crying after a session of lovemaking, it is likely the Ozzie will be blamed for some aspect of the sexual experience. It is very common for the Ozzie to be blamed for the constant mood swings. As a result the Ozzie will begin to internalize the blame, and begin to accept responsibility for it by believing that they actually did something wrong.

7) Chronic feelings of emptiness.

Lacking a sense of self, a person with BPD does not possess the ability to know what fulfilled them. How can they be fulfilled if they have no idea what they want or what makes them happy? Although, they may seek to be happy, desire to be happy, and take steps towards happiness, the sad result is that they rarely succeed in finding something that can fill the emotional black hole in their personality. As a result the person with BPD becomes dismayed, lethargic, and goes into a low-grade form of misery (the fancy term is Dysphoria). They feel empty, void of meaning, and void of substance.

Another root cause of their emptiness is their inability to establish intimacy with the people they care about the most. As a result of splitting, and the tug-of-war with the Ozzie's emotions, there will come a time when the intimacy between the two people will begin to dissipate (if it ever existed). The person with BPD's idolization of the Ozzie will begin to wear off. This will create a feeling of emptiness for the person with BPD because much of their identity is mirroring (copying) desirable behaviors and traits from the Ozzie. As the Ozzie is split "black" and their behaviors, and traits, are no longer seen as positive or desirable, the person with

BPD is left without a source to emulate and build their identity from…they are left empty.

9) Transient, stress related paranoid ideations or severe dissociative symptoms.

Periods of high stress are going to bring out the very worst of this disorder in your loved one. When under extreme pressure and stress the person with BPD could experience dissociation and paranoia. Each carries with them an element of the person separating from the current world and entering the realm of their warped mind where logic, reason, and support will have absolutely no positive impact on their beliefs. In fact, trying to be rational and logical with a paranoid person may result in them directing their skewed perceptions towards you. You will be viewed as the threat that is trying to deceive and control them through your mental manipulations.

So what is Dissociation and Paranoia as it pertains to BPD? Dissociation is when the person with BPD will no longer be responding to the situation, circumstances, or environment before them. Rather, their emotional responses and anger is being triggered and caused by a past traumatic event that caused them great pain. As a result they may exhibit strange behaviors or responses that make no sense to the Ozzie, since the Ozzie is trying to address the current crisis, not past emotional issues. During episodes where the person with BPD dissociates (usually during full blown rage behavior), it is likely they will have a form of amnesia where they will later not remember the behaviors they engaged in or the hurtful things they said. To the person with BPD, the incident never happened, and there will be no convincing them otherwise. If you try to speak to them later about the behavior, chances are you will get a blank stare with denials. Further, the person with BPD may actually accuse you of being the person that engaged in the negative behaviors (Projection).

Paranoia is a temporary irrational belief by the person with BPD that someone, or something, is trying to harm them. This would range from accusing you of trying to physically harm them, thinking someone is trying to poison them, accusing you of having affairs, etc, despite the objections and honest denials of the Ozzie.

In my case, my wife woke me up at 2:00am to confront me, and accuse me of molesting our children. She further accused me of being a master hypnotist that had the ability to control her and our children with a wink of an eye, or snap of my fingers. Her paranoia escalated to a level that she viewed me as a form of super villain, with the capabilities of mind control (another Projection indicating that she felt she did not have control over herself).

Despite your denials, the person with BPD is going to believe what their warped mind tells them to believe. Ultimately it was my wife's paranoia, in conjunction with her BPD, that resulted in my leaving the marriage for both: my children's and my own safety.

As an Ozzie it is important that you educate and familiarize yourself with the hurdles you are faced with. You must learn about the BPD traits, not because you want to be nosey and intrude on the treatment of the person that you care about. That will just lead to obsessing over the disorder. You do not learn about BPD traits because you want to try to fix the person you care about. You must remind yourself that you did not cause this disorder, nor can you fix it. You learn about these traits because, as an Ozzie, your behaviors play a role in the interactions between you and the person with BPD. There is a reason the person with BPD sought you out, and now holds onto you with a death grip. It is this interaction, and your part of it, that you must address if you are going to get out of Oz. You must explore; what does the person with BPD receive from their interaction with you? And more importantly, what do you, the Ozzie, receive from the interactions with the person with BPD?

Chapter 3

The Ozzie Tinman Story

Chapter 3

The Ozzie Tinman Story

So what are my credentials for writing this book? Am I a doctor or therapist that specializes in BPD? Have I taken any special training in treating a person with BPD? Am I a college professor that has committed his life to research and publishing my findings? The answer is "no" to all of the above.

I am a regular person just like you, basing his knowledge from real life experiences and information that I, myself, sought because I found myself in the same black hole that you are in. As many would say, I went to The School of Hard Knocks. Many of these experiences you are having yourself, and as you read, light bulbs are going to go off in your head as you think, "yeah, me too!" This is commonly referred to as the Light Bulb Effect in Ozzie social circles, because these situations help you realize that you are not alone in this battle, and other people can relate to your experiences.

But I would like to share with you some of my background and what experiences led me to becoming the Captain of Air Kansas.

I was raised in a two parent household, and had two sisters and one brother. For the most part my upbringing was traditional and happy. I had a close relationship with my siblings, was a mama's boy at times, and was close to my father through common interests in sports and other male bonding situations. I do recall times when my parents argued over things like money matters, but my memories of this were not until my teens, and even then my parents tried to be respectful to us children by arguing when they thought we could not hear them (but we could) after we went to bed. However, we were a "normal" family, with normal problems, but always knew that each of us were there for one another for love and support at any time.

As I grew and matured, I experienced many achievements in athletics and academics. I felt as though I was confident in my abilities and could take on the world. I excelled in baseball and received offers to continue playing after high school, I was the first person in my family to go to college, and it seemed like every hurdle I came to I leaped over with little effort.

In college I met my future wife when she asked me out on a date through one of her friends. I was already familiar with who she was as her friend was dating one of my best friends. I was flattered and agreed to meet and go on a date with her. Upon meeting her I was taken by her wild spirit and zest for life. She seemed confident and ready to live life to its fullest. Me, being someone that has a fairly subdued personality, was instantly attracted to what she offered: a world of new experiences, carefree times, and having a tour guide to show me these new things.

In total I dated my wife for four years, and we married after we graduated from college, both with Psychology degrees. During our dating period I noticed some red flags in her personality that caused me concern, such as: horrible arguments she would have with her father, the rate at which she would make and dispose of friends, very harsh comments she would make about people she didn't like, her demanding of specific materialistic items, and her neediness for being saved anytime she was under stress (I wrote most of her term papers for her). Yes, I know what you are thinking, "why didn't you cease the relationship with all those red flags?" Honestly, because the negative behaviors that she displayed occurred far enough apart that they could always be explained as "having a bad day", "being tired" or some other reason for being on edge. Further, there was part of me that liked to come in and be the knight in shining armor when she needed saving. This would usually result in her showing great levels of happiness and acceptance of me.

We got married in September of 1995 and I noticed immediate changes in how my wife viewed me. She immediately began buying clothes that she thought presented the "right image for someone of my education." She began to compare us to other married couples, and insisted that we keep up with their material purchases. She would make comments about how I educated myself to the point that I was now better than my extended family. It became a full-time task to present an image of perfection to the world. In order to accommodate the cost of this, I secured two full-time jobs. However, I believed that "making my wife happy" was my job as a husband, and I was willing to do anything to achieve that. It seemed to work because as I achieved and provided everything for her, she showed great levels of appreciation and happiness. Despite my relentless work schedule, I was happy knowing that she was happy.

During this time my wife still experienced difficulties with her father in which she would get into yelling matches with him and refuse to talk to him for months. I did all I could to put fires out between them, when I could, and tried to keep the peace in the extended family.

In June of 1997 we had our first child, a boy. Immediately upon bringing him home, my wife started to show signs of paranoia with a constant urge to protect our child. She began to have concerns that there was someone sneaking in our home at night, and she constantly locked all of the windows and doors. She would have delusions that she saw shadows in our hallway, which indicated to her that we did have an intruder that regularly came into our home at night. Despite my getting up, looking around the house, showing her that all the locks were secure, installing an alarm system, and a security gate on the front door, she continued to believe there was an intruder. When our son was approximately a year and a half old, she ran to me in a panic claiming my son had stopped breathing, was having a seizure, and was turning blue. I called 911 and the paramedics immediately came and took my son to the hospital. All tests performed on him failed to show any abnormality in his breathing or indications that he had a seizure. On more than one occasion my wife called me at work claiming that people were trying to get into our home. I would instruct her to call the police and I would be right home from work. Upon arrival the police always informed me that there was no evidence to support what my wife was claiming. My wife also started to pull away from my extended family claiming they were unsafe. She expressed concerns that my 8-year-old nephew, that I was very close with, was jealous of our son and would try to hurt him. As a result, I pulled away from my nephew, thus leaving him without a positive male role model in his life. It seemed that there was always a crisis and chaos that surrounded my wife, with little or no evidence to suggest that her panic and severe responses were appropriate.

While my son was still very young, my wife began to ask for another child because, "she felt whole and it made her happy to be pregnant." I initially resisted because I had recognized that my wife was having some mental health difficulties. I was no doctor, but when the person you love is exhibiting odd and paranoid behaviors, your gut has a way of sending warnings to your heart and head. I refused to have another child for a year at which time I caved to the pressure from my wife, and extended family, to "just have one more." My wife became pregnant almost immediately after we started trying.

During her pregnancy with our second child, her paranoia continued to escalate. She became very withdrawn from me and all intimacy was lost in the relationship. Sexual contact was brought to a minimum, approximately once every two or three months, and any physical contact was met with resistance by her. She was now pregnant and my job as a sperm donor was complete. There was no reason for sexual contact. She also started to accuse me of having affairs, sneaking out at night, harboring pornography, and being deceptive. As a result of her constant rejection, accusations, and the pain I felt, I began to withdraw emotionally from her. I eventually lost interest in going to bed with her and would stay up late at night watching television. I started staying on the computer, writing emails to friends and family, and surfing the internet just to fill time. I began writing editorial articles for various websites on pretty much any subject I could use my time to research about. I brought work home and contributed many hours to my employer that I never sought payment for (however, I did win the Officer of the Year Award that year).

Approximately 6 months into her pregnancy the accusations became escalated and the "Rages" began. She would yell, scream, and belittle me, and tell me what a disappointment I had become. She would accuse me of trying to intentionally hurt her and make her life miserable. All I could do was deny and tell her that I too felt betrayed by her rejections. Yet not once did she acknowledge that she had contributed to the situation we had found ourselves in. It was all my fault, and I began to believe her.

Our second child was born in October of 1999, a girl. After the birth, my wife would have long intervals in which she would alternate between loving and adoring me, and completely hating and mistrusting me. I was constantly trying to figure out which woman I would come home to from work. Would I get a kiss at the front door, or an emotional right cross to the kisser? I had no idea until I walked in the door. However, since her periods of alternating between love and hate became farther apart, I enjoyed the happy times, and trudged forward through the difficult times, figuring I had an obligation to my wife and children to make the marriage work. However, during the bad periods, my wife's paranoia, delusions, and hostility continued. I was lost in the Fear of the situation, Obligation to my family, and the Guilt of wanting something better for myself and my children. The Fear, Obligation, and Guilt an Ozzie feels is often referred to as FOG in the BPD support community. The years passed by and my wife's behavior was getting more openly hostile and angry. She had cut off all sexual relations and seemed to only agree when she reached the point that she had concerns that I would have an affair if she continued to reject me. By that time sex became about a tension and biological outlet, rather than any intimate sharing of love and trust. I could have been having sex with anyone and received the same primal gratification. Night after night she would rage at me, yell at me, throw herself on the ground, and accuse me of trying to destroy her life. All along I still constantly attempted to prove to her that I still loved her. I fell into the habit of gift giving, because it provided for short periods in which she would show satisfaction with me. I agreed to buy a house I didn't like, filled with beautiful furniture, rare art, a new SUV, and pretty much any material item that she asked for. The moments of "happiness" that she displayed were short-lived, and financially expensive. But I constantly tried to "make her happy" by doing anything and everything she asked. I blamed myself for her constant misery.

By the end of 2003 my wife had become overbearingly controlling to the point that anything in the household that was not done in the manner that she specified was met with harsh consequences. These consequences were normally being kept awake all night long while she relentlessly verbally attacked me to the point that I broke down in tears. She would then accuse me of trying to be manipulative and verbally attacked me more for having the nerve to cry in front of her. I can still hear her in my head yelling, "be a man!" as I sit here writing. By the end of 2003 she had also managed to isolate me from my extended family because she decided that my relatives were all too dangerous to be around our children. Trying to keep the peace in my immediate family, I did like a good Ozzie and let her have her way.

Valentine's Day, 2004, was the defining point where I began my journey to Kansas. On that day my wife came home and told me that she had forgotten to buy a Valentine's Day present for me and the kids, and that we were going to skip presents that year. I told her "no problem", and that I understood she had busy days that did not allow her to always get everything done. So I went to work like usual. While I was at work I decided I would take the day off, go shopping, and surprise her and the kids with some Valentine's gifts. I went to Victoria Secrets and bought her some new flannel pajamas, I went to the Disney Store and bought the kids some stuffed animals, then stopped at the flower store on the way home and picked up some flowers for my wife and daughter. That evening after dinner I gave my wife the pajamas, and the kids their dolls (from both me and their mother). It was a fun time and I was happy with how the evening went. That was until the children went to bed. After they fell asleep my wife immediately attacked me. She accused me of trying to show her up in front of the children, trying to "control" Valentine's Day, and how I made her feel like a bad wife because I bought her a gift. She told me how I was a terrible person, how deceptive I was, how I could never be trusted, and how much she hated me. For six hours she relentlessly pounded me emotionally. I resorted to begging her to stop as I was bent over holding my stomach and crying (for a visual, I am 6'3", 215lbs, and my wife was 5'6", 110lbs). She was merciless telling me how I deserved this treatment for betraying her, and despite my begging, she continued until she herself was exhausted. When she was done, she looked me in the eye and told me that everything was my fault, and said she wanted to make an appointment with a marriage therapist to straighten me out. In desperation to save the marriage I agreed to go to marriage therapy. The next day I made an appointment for the beginning of March.

We went to our first appointment and my wife played victim. She cried in front of the therapist (keep in mind I had never seen my wife cry before this other than the birth of our children), claimed that I emotionally abused her, and that I was a tyrant towards her and the children. I was in absolute control and she was a weak victim just trying to make it from day to day. I adamantly disagreed and told the therapist that her accounts were not accurate. She cried harder calling me a bully. That was our first session and we were scheduled for another session in a week.

During that week my wife avoided me like the plague. She refused to sit in the same room together and spoke very little. That was until the night before our next session. That night she woke me up at 2:00am, looked at me, and told me that she had figured out what was wrong in our home. I will never forget her words as they are etched in my memory, "You are molesting our children, just admit it!" I adamantly denied, yet she had made up her mind. For 4 hours she questioned me about anything I had done with our children, with me denying absolutely everything. For good measure, she also accused my brother and cousin of molesting the children. In addition, she attempted to get me to say my father had molested me. Again, I denied because it was not true. But she "knew."

The next day we went into our therapy session and she formally accused me of molesting our children in front of the therapist. The therapist asked me if I would be willing to agree to a polygraph test (lie detector) and I agreed. That night she left our home with the kids until I could arrange and take the test. Five days later, and at the cost of $500, I took the lie detector test, which showed I had not done anything to our children. I will never forget the embarrassment and humiliation, and sickening feeling in my stomach as I sat there while the examiner asked me if I sexually molested my children. It is something I will carry with me for the rest of my life. But again, at that time I was deeply lost in Oz and desperate to save my marriage. I still wanted to prove to my wife that she could trust me, and we continued our marriage therapy.

A month passed and the therapist asked me to come into his office for a private session. At that time he informed me that my wife had been diagnosed with Borderline Personality Disorder, and that she was a very sick woman. He also gave me the book, "I Hate You, Don't Leave Me" and told me that the best thing I could do was educate myself about her disorder, because it was not going to get better anytime soon. He also informed me that he was going to slow our marriage therapy to one session every three or four weeks, and he wanted to see my wife alone to deal with her disorder. I agreed.

Nine months passed in therapy and my wife made little progress. Her therapist claimed to me that she was making great strides in her treatment; however, our home was still every bit as unstable and chaotic as the day we walked in his door. In many respects it had gotten worse, as she became openly hostile towards me in front of the children and would make statements such as, "just seeing you enrages me." She also accused me of being a master hypnotist because she found some old hypnosis cassette tapes I bought off Ebay a couple of year prior just out of curiosity. In her mind, this justified her claim that I

was secretly hypnotizing her and the children to
control them. My wife refused to take her
prescribed medications that were offered to her by
the therapist to control her paranoia and delusions,
and continued to rage at me on a regular basis. By
this time she had also completely isolated me from
our children to the point that I had to ask her for
permission to play with them. Even then she would
supervise our interactions the whole time while
making comments that I was being controlling and
mean to them. During this period the therapist
would assure me that things would get better and to
"hang in there."

Approximately two months into couple's therapy I
did what any good Ozzie would do by consuming
myself with trying to learn about my wife's disorder
so I could "fix it." In doing so, I found a wealth of
information on the internet including support
groups, websites dedicated to information about
BPD and Ozzies, and good people willing to share
their experiences and advice. Little by little, I came
to discover that I had no control over my wife's
disorder: I did not cause it, I could not fix it, and
that my way to Kansas was through myself taking
care of me. I could not get to Kansas by trying to
drag my wife along and forcing her to get better.
That was out of my realm of control. I could only
control myself, my own actions, and ultimately my
own destiny. When I realized this AND accepted it,
I began to see that there was hope…for me. If there

was hope for my wife, she would have to discover it, and do the hard work to achieve it on her own.

As the months passed I became stronger and more confident in my ability to face my issues. I learned about my wife's disorder, not because I wanted to fix her (my original motive) but because I wanted to address my own behaviors that served a definite role in the unhealthy relationship. I used internet support groups to share my experiences, receive validation, and at times to get a reality check when I started to slide back into Oz thinking. I reconnected with my extended family, focused on meeting my children's needs, and fulfilling my parental role without any strings attached. I put up boundaries and refused to tolerate abuse from my wife any longer. During this time she kicked and screamed about the changes I was implementing, claiming I was being controlling and had abandoned all of her needs. She was right. I was now controlling my life and destiny. I had abandoned the role of knight in shining armor and was now refusing to take responsibility and blame for her inappropriate behaviors.

As my wife realized that I was making positive strides in my own mental and physical health, her BPD behavior began to escalate greatly. After all, if I was healthy and well, she had no one else to blame for the situation except for herself. The rules were changing and she no longer had someone who would blindly take care of her every whim and request. She panicked and went back into crisis. However, by November 2004, I no longer felt the FOG (fear, obligation and guilt) to tolerate her abuse. I no longer stayed and gave her an audience when she threw herself on the ground and pounded the floor. I no longer argued back when she made outlandish accusations against me. I had taken back control of my self-worth and dignity that I deserved. As a result of her world and rules being turned upside down, she again resorted to the one thing she knew would hurt me the most in an attempt to get a response.

On November 15, 2004, she accused me again of molesting our children. At that time I calmly informed her that I would be leaving the marriage and would not be returning. That night I packed my belongings and drove away knowing that I would never allow my wife to hurt me again. That night I stood up, refused to be abused, and promised myself that I would never get lost in the FOG again. That night I saw clearly and placed the futures of my children and myself first by completing my journey to Kansas.

It has been 5 months since I left my wife, and I am currently in the process of a divorce. My resolve to stay in Kansas is every bit as strong today as it was the day that I left. Within these last 5 months I have noticed a distinct difference in my children, the joy that they express when they are with me, and the self-gratification I can take in our growth. I am proud of myself for what I am becoming and look forward to what the future holds for me and my children. What does the future hold for my wife? That is up to her to decide and resolve. In the meantime, I will bask in the green grass of Kansas, look at the blue sky, and appreciate my size 13 Ruby Red Slippers.

Chapter 4

An Honest Look
At Yourself

Chapter 4

An Honest Look At Yourself

A vital part of escaping Oz is taking responsibility for your own issues that play a role in the relationship between the Ozzie and person with BPD. It is easy for an Ozzie to latch onto the fact that the person with BPD has a diagnosis and try to saddle that person with all of the responsibility for the failure of their relationship. By doing so you are punishing your significant other for having a disorder, rather than taking an honest look at yourself and admitting that you too had a role in the direction that your relationship went.

There are many Ozzies that educate themselves, go through the steps of grieving a lost relationship, and follow through with leaving the person diagnosed with BPD. Then a year later, the same person returns back to the BPD community to share that they have once again built a relationship with another person with BPD. How could this happen? It's very simple. The Ozzie may have left their first sick relationship in search of greener pastures. However, they remained in Oz because they never addressed their own responsibility in the original relationship, nor did they change any of their own unhealthy behaviors that attracted them to the person with BPD, and vice versa. As a result, they end up in the exact same situation that they tried to leave. Rather than taking responsibility for themselves and making the needed changes, they choose to saddle the person with BPD with all the blame and responsibility. Thus, they fail to make any personal growth of their own and repeat the same mistakes.

In order to take back control of your life and escape Oz, the Ozzie must address specific behaviors in their own personality. They need to be able to recognize when they are sending out signals to a person with BPD that screams, "Hey look at me! I am willing to be taken advantage of!" The Ozzie also needs to recognize that they were attracted to the person with BPD and what they sought to gain from the unhealthy dynamic. This chapter will focus on the common issues an Ozzie must face about themselves and overcome during their recovery.

Stop Trying To Fix The Person With BPD: What was the first thing you did when you discovered that the person you cared about was diagnosed with BPD? If you did what I did, the first thing you did was seek all the information you could get to "help" the person you care about get better. You searched high and low, far and wide, for any information you could take home and utilize to fix your loved one's disorder. This is a huge mistake. Basically what you are doing is perpetuating the exact same behavior that keeps you in Oz. You are trying to be the knight in shining armor that rides in on their white horse to save the person you love. You are trying to save the helpless person and take responsibility for their happiness. You are trying to CONTROL another person and their emotional responses. What you should be doing is focusing on yourself and making the changes in you to address your own contribution to the unhealthy relationship. Rather, you choose to focus your attention on someone else so that you are distracted enough to not have to focus on yourself.

During this period of change and confusion, you have to do the exact opposite of what your instincts as an Ozzie tell you to do. Rather than riding in to rescue the person you care about, like you want to, you have to back away from them and allow the person to take responsibility for their own behaviors, mental health, and growth. It is the only way the person with BPD will be able to address their personality issues and changes what they need to make. If you continuously interject in their treatment and attempt to save them, you are creating a roadblock. The person with BPD will be more than happy to allow you to continue your old behavior and save them. It is one of the reasons that they sought you out from everyone else in the world. If it is your responsibility to save them, then they have no responsibility to get themselves better.

There is a saying among Ozzies that you are going to hear time and time again. It goes: "You did not cause this disorder. You cannot fix it. It is not your responsibility." An Ozzie must learn to completely separate themself from the treatment of the person with BPD, and allow the person to be responsible for their own decisions, behavior and consequences. It is very hard to do, but it's necessary for the mental health of both, you and the person you care about.

In regards to learning about BPD and things that you do that interact with the disorder, constantly give yourself checks and balances. When taking an action, ask yourself if your intentions are for your own personal growth or if you are trying to do something to fix or help the person with BPD. If your intentions are to in some way control, or assist, the person with BPD, reassess your actions and refocus where you are placing your energy. If you come to the conclusion that your actions are with the intent of addressing your own issues and unhealthy behaviors then you are on the right track.

Take Responsibility For Yourself: Even though the person with BPD will constantly accuse you of things that you have not done, there will come a time that they will actually be right, and are justifiably angry. In such a situation own up to your wrongs and take responsibility. Too often Ozzies are so gun shy from being constantly attacked that they begin to deny, deny, and when all else fails, deny some more. It is common for Ozzies to fall into a habit of lying as a result of fear, and as a means of trying to avoid the harsh angry responses of the person with BPD. What will eventually happen is that the person with BPD will start to do their research before they approach you. They will actually know that you have done something that you should not have done, but will question you to see if you own up to your responsibility. Then when you deny, "ah hah!", they have you backed into a corner. Next thing you know, not only have you legitimately done something wrong that they were already angry about, but you have just proven yourself to be untrustworthy and deceitful in their perceptions. They will not understand that your denials were out of fear. They will only understand that you have been dishonest and therefore are not deserving of their trust. You have contributed to their "splitting" of you.

Voluntarily Climb Off The Pedestal: There will be times when the person with BPD will adore you. They will tell you how much they love you, tell friends and family how great you are, and hold you high on the pedestal for the world to see. And yes, it will feel wonderful while it lasts. But the reality of the situation is that just as the person with BPD will split you white, they will also eventually split you black. And the severity in which you are split will likely be just as strong, but in the opposite direction. So if you are split white to the point that your loved one is worshipping and deifying you, then guess what…when you are split black you will become one with Satan himself, and your life will become a living hell.

The only way to avoid these extreme splits is to voluntarily refuse to be on the pedestal. When you recognize that your loved one is over-complimenting you, is acting as though you are perfect, and expressing undeserved high praise, verbally tell them that you are uncomfortable being placed on a pedestal. Tell them that although you appreciate the compliments, that what you did does not warrant such high praise, and you behaved as anyone else would have in the same situation. Bring yourself down a level or two, and politely decline the extreme compliment so that their image of you remains grounded in reality.

By voluntarily climbing off the pedestal you are possibly defusing a severe split. Yes, you will still experience being split, but you will be working proactively to lessen the severity of the pendulum swing when it occurs.

Drop The Mentality Of A Victim: Ozzies will fall into a pattern of feeling sorry for themselves and adopt the identity of a victim. And yes, due to the emotional, verbal, and sometimes physical abuse, that we sustain, every single one of us can justifiably claim that we are victims. However, keeping this mentality only keeps us trapped in Oz because with being a victim comes being powerless and a lack of control. This is exactly the response that the person with BPD wants us to display as a means of keeping us off balance. Escaping from Oz will require you to be a Lion and recapture the power, control and courage to not be a victim. Escaping Oz will require that you refuse to tolerate unacceptable behavior and stand up for your boundaries. You can't do this while you are being a victim.

As you go through the process of healing and growing, there will be times that you feel weak and helpless. This is normal in short intervals during times of change. As a Lion you must be willing to face these fears and doubts, and know that you will overcome them. You must remain firm in your resolve to not fall back into being the victim, no matter how hard the person with BPD tries to force you back into the role. Stand firm and strong, and constantly tell yourself that you are not a victim, you are a survivor, you are a Lion.

Don't be afraid to ask for help, especially if you are being subjected to physical violence. Sometimes asking for help and exposing your situation can be the most courageous move you can make. Further, it may save your life. Standing firm and refusing to be a victim does not mean placing yourself in danger. It simply means that you will not tolerate the abuse, whether you can do that while remaining in the home, or if you have to leave for your safety.

Recognize Who Truly Is In Control: So who is in control in your relationship? Does the person with BPD call the shots and demand that things be done their way, or else they throw a huge temper tantrum? Do you agree to everything they say and want simply to avoid conflict? These responses by an Ozzie are very common, as we do all we can to keep the relationship as stable as possible. However, what you have done is given your control to the person with BPD. It is your control and you can take it back. The person with BPD will fight tooth and nail to keep you from taking control of yourself back. Maintaining control over you is their source of power in the relationship and is a necessary tool for them to hoover (suck) you back time and time again.

So how do you take control back? Repeat after me, "No." Okay, let's try that again. You didn't sound like you meant it. Here we go again, "No." And one more time, "No." Sometimes an Ozzie taking control of themselves can be as simple as saying, "No" when they do not feel like agreeing to the unrealistic demands of the person with BPD. However, as Ozzies, we feel like it is our duty to do everything our loved one asks of us as our means of showing that we care about them. After all, we want to feel needed and important, and what better way than to go out of our way to make the person we love happy. The problem with this belief is that it is unhealthy for us to constantly be willing to give and drain ourselves emotionally, without ever demanding that our partner return anything into our emotional gas tank. Eventually we begin to feel taken advantage of and build resentment. Plus many of the demands that the person with BPD makes are so unrealistic, or difficult to accomplish that we set ourselves up to fail in both, ours and the person with BPD's eyes.

I remember in one of my first individual therapy sessions the therapist asked me if I ever agreed to something for my wife that I strongly opposed to. I brought up the subject of my wife buying our second house and how I told her multiple times that I did not like the house, and wanted to stay in our current home we were already in. However, she pursued negotiations for the house behind my back, and before I knew what happened she put us in a position where the seller was relying on us to buy their home. Then despite my disapproval, I agreed to buy the house. My therapist looked me dead in the eye and asked, "why didn't you just say 'no'? Why didn't you just refuse to sign the purchase papers?" It hit me like a ton of bricks. Up until that moment I had always felt powerless to say "no" to anything my wife wanted. But at that moment I realized that all along I did have the control and power, if I chose to utilize it. I had given complete control and power to my wife simply because I never realized that saying "no" was an option. It sounds like common sense, but refusing to do something you don't want to do is very empowering and a key ingredient to taking control of your life back.

Self Blaming: We Ozzies are so used to hearing the person with BPD blame us, accuse us, and tell us that everything is our fault, we begin to actually believe them. We start to believe that if only we did something different, said something different, or adjusted our behavior in some way, the person we care about would not be so hostile towards us. We begin to take responsibility for their anger and internalize it as something that we caused and have control over. The truth of the matter is that a person with BPD responds to us with hostility not because we did something bad, but because they feel so bad about themselves. Many times the hostile response has absolutely nothing to do with us, even though the person with BPD is able to point to some obscure incident involving you to claim you are the root of the anger.

Ozzies need to recognize that they did not cause or create the person's Borderline Personality Disorder condition. Yes, the person may tell you that you caused their pain or their disorder, but you need to understand that it is not true. The person with BPD is a confused person looking for someone to blame for their circumstances. Since you are the person that is right in front of them and so emotionally close that you are unlikely to leave them, you become the emotional punching bag. Despite their hostility towards you, accusations that everything is your fault, and constant belittling, you must keep in mind that you are not to blame. Refuse to take responsibility for their condition or anger, and place responsibility back where it belongs, on the person with BPD.

What Kind Of Treatment And Medication Is Your Loved One On?: You are going to hear Ozzies asking all the time, "Is your partner using DBT (Dialectic Behavior Therapy)? Are they in regular group therapy? Are they on medication?" Quite frankly, should it matter to the Ozzie?

The treatment and medication being used by the person with BPD is their own concern and responsibility, not yours. However, curiosity and concern for the person you care about often leads the Ozzie to interject themselves into finding out what the treatment plan is. Is it really your business or are you just again focusing on the person with BPD rather than yourself?

Say for example your significant other has a therapist that is open to sharing the treatment plan. He tells you what therapy techniques are being used, what medications are being taken, and updates you on the progress of the person with BPD. What good does that do for you and your own progress? What if you disagree with the treatment or medications? Is the therapist going to change their treatment plan because you, a layman, disagrees with their professional treatment? Absolutely not.

So what would be the purpose of you enmeshing yourself in the treatment of your loved one, other than to be nosey or to distract yourself from your own issues?

The proof if their treatment is effective or not is truly in the results that you observe in your interactions. Is the person with BPD trying to control their outbursts? Are they taking steps to de-escalate themselves and find positive outlets for their anger? Have suicide attempts or self-mutilation lessened or ceased? Are they becoming more self-reliant? This is the proper place for you, the Ozzie, to observe if treatment is effective, as this is where you are personally being affected.

There are two exception in which it is appropriate for the Ozzie to interject in the treatment. One, if the person with BPD is given an ultimatum to seek and start treatment or the Ozzie is leaving the relationship. In that case it is appropriate for the Ozzie to check if the person is in compliance with their treatment to insure the safety of the Ozzie and any children. Next is if the person with BPD begins to self-harm. Then it is appropriate for the Ozzie to contact their therapist and report the behavior.

Codependency: Ozzies are notoriously people that display codependent traits in a relationship. What is codependency? In a nutshell, a codependent person is someone that constantly sacrifices themselves for the happiness of another person despite never being rewarded for their sacrifices. As a result the person begins to feel taken advantage of and resentful towards the person they are constantly sacrificing themselves for. It is a very destructive force in a relationship because the codependent person will always give more then they receive back, and will eventually get to the point that they completely shut down emotionally because they feel taken advantage of and like their needs are not being met. The codependent person will set up situations where they play the martyr and fall into the victim role.

Codependent people tend to be givers, and are constantly striving to receive acceptance, approval, and love by providing those they care about with everything they ask for. In the process of completely sacrificing themselves, codependent people end up losing themselves and their identities, as they redefine themselves as an emotional and physical servant to the person they are focused on. They voluntarily take on the role and some Ozzies will even wear their codependency like a badge of honor, as a means of showing the world just how much they "give."

During a session, my therapist asked me what my role in the relationship was. I proudly said, "I am the provider." When the therapist asked me exactly what that meant, I told her, "I give the people that I care for, my family, what they need and ask for." When she asked how do I determine what I am able to give, I responded, "I try to give them anything they ask for. If they are asking for it, then it must be important to them. I want to provide the people that I love with the things that are important to them." She then asked me, when do I stop giving? My answer, "When I feel taken advantage of." Yep, you guessed it. You are looking at a recovering codependent. I am recovering in the sense that I recognize my codependent behaviors and traits when they arise, and avoid the urge to give as a means of gaining acceptance and love.

Codependency becomes extremely destructive in an Ozzie and BPD relationship because of the dynamics are such that you have an extreme giver matched with an extreme taker. The relationship is doomed to fail unless both partners recognize their destructive traits and change them. What will commonly happen is that the Ozzie will constantly give, emotionally and physically, in the desperate attempt to gain acceptance and love from the person with BPD. Since the person with BPD has a great fear of intimacy, they are incapable of returning the love and acceptance that the Ozzie is seeking. As a result, the Ozzie will give until they are emotionally empty. Further the person with BPD will resent the Ozzie when they have nothing left to give, emotionally or physically, as over time they will develop a sense of entitlement to what the Ozzie has been giving them.

I've Got Fleas!: In any relationship, when two people are around each other for a great deal of time they begin to adopt certain characteristics from one another. They adopt beliefs, attitudes, and responses. This becomes troublesome in a relationship between an Ozzie and someone with BPD, as the Ozzie will find themselves beginning to utilize Borderline responses as an acceptable form of communication/expression. So instead of having one person yelling and raging, you now have two people doing it to each other. Ozzies refer to this as "Having or Catching Fleas." It is the process in which an Ozzie's thought process becomes distorted and they begin to accept Borderline responses as normal. The Ozzie, in a sense, adopts BPD.

Even more troubling than an Ozzie catching fleas, is when children in the household begin to accept BPD behavior as normal and acceptable. Children can begin the process of developing BPD by initially catching flea, and learning that the destructive behaviors work for them as a means to get the things they want. As they grow, the children engrain this warped belief system of responses into their personality, and BPD becomes a learned disorder for them. As the healthy parent your job is to keep your children grounded firmly in Kansas and teach them logical and rational responses. The consequences for failing to do this are huge, as later you may discover that you have lost your child to this disorder. Whether you can keep your child grounded in Kansas while maintaining your marriage relationship, or if you have to leave to provide them a safe and stable home, is going to be a decision that you must face during your own recovery process.

Keep in mind the old saying, "Treat others as you want to be treated." This will help keep you in the proper frame of mind to resist catching fleas. A person with BPD may treat you with no respect or dignity, but ask yourself if this is the person who's behaviors you wish to emulate? Or do you want to be a better, healthier person, who is a positive role model for your children and family?

If you find yourself responding to the person with BPD with the same disrespect, hostility, and meanness that they display, then you know you need a good flea dip. Get rid of those behaviors before they take over and become part of your engrained defense mechanisms.

Kansas vs. Oz: In your journey to recovery you will have to face the fact that your perceptions of reality are distorted. Many Ozzies begin their journey only to find out that their perceptions have been twisted and turned so many times that they are left in absolute confusion. As a result they go running back to Oz out of fear of having to face a world they are not familiar with. Although Oz is chaotic, stressful, and painful, at least Oz is familiar.

Over time you have been exposed to the person with BPD, their logic, rationale, and interpretations of the world. After a while you begin to get sucked into their way of thinking, their perceptions of the world, and their belief system. What they say begins to make sense to you, although other people around you always seem to express that they view things far differently. Being firmly in Oz you view the world through fragmented glasses in which only pieces of reality can be seen, while the rest is a jumbled mess. In order to complete your trip to Kansas you must be willing to put the proper set of glasses on that will bring reality and your perceptions into proper focus.

Common ways in which a person with BPD may distort your reality is by altering your beliefs that will result in your isolation. They will tell you that members of your family are mean and destructive. They will present "facts" and splinters of the truth to prove their point. If you listen long enough you may begin to believe what they are telling you and start to separate from extended family members, thus isolating yourself from them. When you start to recover, you will discover that what you thought was reality is actually riddled with lies, distortions, and exaggerations. Facing this realization is scary as you begin to find that so much of what you thought existed was only figments of the imagination of the person with BPD. You are then faced with having to reconstruct what truly is reality, and separate Kansas from Oz.

The Truth Shall Set You Free: There are many things that happen within the confines of your home that are embarrassing, hurtful, and uncomfortable to share. As a result you hide what is happening, you protect the person with BPD by pretending the behaviors do not exist, and you work overtime to present an image of the "perfect family" while interacting with friends and family. You are the envy of all your friends and family as they are constantly fed this belief that you have everything you ever sought: the perfect spouse, the perfect children, and the perfect home with a white picket fence. However, behind this wonderfully manufactured image you are dying inside having to conceal what is truly happening in your life. You live a lie and you know it. The image that you work so hard to portray is nothing more than a mask concealing the volcano that lies beneath. But you continue to perpetrate this mirage out of Fear, Obligation, and Guilt, that people will truly discover the horrors that you and your children live with on a daily basis.

The pressure that you place on yourself to maintain this image and lie is truly stifling. You end up making decisions based upon what fits best into your public persona rather than what is best for you and your children. Forbid the thought that you acknowledge things are not completely harmonious in your home. People might actually gain insight to the fact that you and your children are being abused, and that your spouse is mentally ill. You go into

"Protect Mode" promising yourself that you will never disclose the secrets and skeletons that lie behind the closed doors of your home.

In order to maintain this image and to conceal your skeletons, you will eventually have to disconnect from your emotions. You will have to place all the negative emotions connected to the abuse you are being subjected to in the back of your head and pretend to be happy and put together in public. As you repress those negative emotions more and more, you will become withdrawn, depressed, and start to lose yourself in your fantasy world as you lie to yourself thinking that things "are not that bad."

After a while these lies and distortions that you work so hard to maintain will become a weight that you must carry all the time. What was once a little white lie becomes a monkey on your back. Eventually that monkey becomes an elephant that is crushing you. The only way to get rid of this weight is to break the cycle of lies and share with people you trust what is truly happening in your home. And here is the kicker…when you tell them, they will reply that they already knew!

In order to receive your passport to Kansas, you have to be willing to let go of the lies and distortions, especially the ones that you contribute to. You have to live in reality. When you let go of these lies and distortions you will feel a huge relief of the burden lifted from you. You can then turn your efforts to living as you truly are. While you go through this process of exposing yourself and your experiences to those you trust, a wonderful thing will happen. Family and friends that you thought would reject you for your faults actually embrace you and provide support.

Poor Personal Boundaries: One of the key dynamics is a relationship between an Ozzie and person with BPD is that both participants have poor personal boundaries. What is a personal boundary? A personal boundary is a limit that a person places on the intrusiveness they will allow by another person. Your boundaries define who you are, and where you end and another person begins. Boundaries define how you allow others to treat you, what you believe, and they protect you from both physical and emotional threats.

In an Ozzie and BPD relationship both partners lack well defined boundaries, and as a result begin to mesh into one person. The Ozzie intrudes on their loved one by defining their life's goal as gratifying and trying to "make" their partner happy. They lose all sense of their self and focus completely on living to serve the person with BPD. The person with BPD intrudes on the Ozzie by placing the burden on them to constantly supply them with emotional stimuli and a surrogate identity, since they do not have a true identity of their own. The Ozzie and person with BPD eventually end up living as

Siamese twins where both are completely dependent and reliant upon each other to provide their lifelines.

The most obvious intrusion is the crossing of emotional barriers. This is where the person with BPD engages in rage behaviors, verbal abuse, emotional blackmail, and other actions that are done as a means to emotionally beat the Ozzie into submission. The Ozzie has weak emotional boundaries so they allow the person with BPD to steam roll over them, again and again. The Ozzie fails to establish a definite line of behavior that they will not tolerate.

On the other hand, the Ozzie is just as intrusive on the emotional boundaries of the person with BPD. The Ozzie wants to be the savior of the person with BPD. They want to come in and take care of all their wants and needs, and many times they do. The result is that the person with BPD becomes completely reliant on the Ozzie to do everything for them. They become helpless and emotionally unable to function because they have no self-worth or confidence to do anything for themselves. In some relationships the lack of physical boundaries crosses into physical abuse. In the course of the rage and hostility that accompanies an Ozzie and BPD relationship, there are situations that could escalate to dangerous levels, where one or both partners resort to violence to establish ultimate control.

The only way to address the violation of weak boundaries is to actually develop, and enforce, stronger boundaries. What behaviors are you willing to tolerate, and which behaviors do you consider to be violations of your person? Boundaries are not up for debate with your partner, as they are YOUR personal boundaries. They should be determined by your own comfort level and what you believe crosses the line between appropriate and inappropriate behavior. Your boundaries must be clear and concise because the person with BPD will test and try to see how firm they are. When you experience this testing you must be willing to stand up for yourself, whether it is verbally telling the person that they will not do something to you, or you may actually have to leave temporarily (or permanently if the violation is severe enough). But your loved one must see that you are serious and that there will be consequences for a violation.

In regards to you violating your loved one's boundaries, you must constantly remind yourself that their disorder is not your responsibility. Recognize the behaviors that are associated with BPD and refuse to take responsibility for them. If the person acts helpless and refuses to do something they are perfectly capable of doing, then guess what: it does not get done. If your loved one rages at you and exhibits inappropriate behavior, leave the room or perhaps the house. You don't have to stand there and accept the abuse and violations of your boundaries. Let them maintain responsibility for their own issues and behaviors. If a physical barrier is crossed through physical abuse, the best advice I can give is to seek help and safety. File a police report so, at a minimum, a paper trail is started in the event the abusive behavior continues. If necessary, arrange to escape the situation entirely. Get yourself away from the physically dangerous threat first and foremost. You can worry about escaping Oz at a later time when your safety is secured.

Chapter 5

Taking Care Of Number 1

Chapter 5

Taking Care Of Number 1

As an Ozzie you have spent a great deal of your time attempting to take care of other people. You believed that the path to have your needs met, receive approval, and receive love, was by giving to others. However, during the time that you ran around trying to make everyone else happy, you forgot one very important person, yourself. Chances are you are reading this book because you are miserable and confused about the circumstances that you find yourself in now. And I am also willing to bet that regardless of all your attempts to run around and make everyone else happy, they are just as unhappy and confused as you are.

In order to be a positive influence on other people's lives, you must first focus on making yourself a happy and content person. This involves building up your self-confidence, social ties, proper health care, and other vital components to your health that you have neglected as you tried feverishly to meet the needs of the person with BPD. However, in order to focus on yourself you must let go of the control that you are trying to exert over the person with BPD in your life. What control you ask? An Ozzie exerts control by trying to determine and alter the emotions their loved one displays. The only person that can decide if the person with BPD in your life will be happy, sad, depressed, etc, is the person with BPD themselves. It is their responsibility, not yours. Okay, so on the count of three, take a breath, open your hands, and let go of trying to control the person with BPD in your life. Ready? 1...2...3. Now, let's focus your attention where it should be, on yourself. In order to get yourself healthy again, physically and mentally, you are going to have to address both your body and your mind. You are going to have to recognize that just as only the person with BPD can make themselves happy, you are the only person that has the control and power to make yourself happy. So what are some ways that you can do that?

Reconnect With Family And Friends: When in a relationship with a person with BPD, their demands become so great that the Ozzie finds all of their time consumed with trying to meet those demands. The partner with BPD may also sabotage the Ozzie's friendships and family relationships as a means of maintaining control over them. After all, the person with BPD can't have the Ozzie socializing too much or else the truth about their abusive behaviors may be revealed. As a result, the Ozzie becomes isolated and cut off from all social interaction that is not monitored by the person with BPD.

When Ozzies begin their journey to Kansas, they are going to need a strong support system. The journey is not easy and will require that the Ozzie have close relationships and support for an emotional outlet that has been forbidden by their partner up to that point. The Ozzie will need to reconnect with family members and friends that they have either voluntarily distanced themselves from or were forbidden to socialize with. The Ozzie needs people they can trust and rely on to share all of the things that have been concealed in their life. This will be their safe haven. It will be where the Ozzie will need to learn how to receive love and support rather than constantly giving.

Support Groups: Support groups are wonderful for receiving validation and reality checks. Groups can be found on the internet as well as face-to-face within your local community. However, pure face-to-face Ozzie, or Non BPD, groups can be difficult to find as they are often combined with Bipolar Nons and other personality disorder Nons. Personally, I preferred the internet groups because the members tend to be very honest in their responses and are available 24 hours a day, seven days a week. Plus it is also a treat to personally speak to some of the well known experts in the BPD community, as many will frequent the groups and serve as moderators (thank you Elyce for all your help and support! I couldn't have made my trip to Kansas without your guidance).

Support groups serve four main functions in your recovery. First, they provide you the validation from other Ozzies that are sharing similar personal experiences. You feel less alone and can receive first hand advice how other Ozzies confronted similar situations. Second, your fellow Ozzies provide you with constant "Reality Checks." From time to time you will fall back into Oz thinking (or Stinkin Thinkin), and will begin to display unhealthy behaviors and emotional responses again. Since many of your fellow Ozzies have fallen into the same traps, they immediately start ringing bells and blowing whistles at you. In a very nice and caring way they will tell you where your head is and let you know that you need to come back to reality. Third, the groups are a great resource of information in which you learn about BPD and how it affects you. Ozzies of all degrees visit the support group. Some of them live in Oz and some live in Kansas, but all are there to provide insight and information about what you are experiencing. Listen to them, they truly know what they are talking about. Some of the more senior Ozzies will give you PhD answers in simple layman terms to help you figure out the technical language that therapists use. And as I said earlier, there are some true clinical experts of BPD that devote their time and energy to the groups, and are very assessable. They always provide great information and guidance, free of charge. Finally, the groups serve as a place that you can vent and share while remaining anonymous. It is a safe place where you do not have to worry about the person with BPD in your life hearing what you are sharing, or fear that what you say will get back to them. We all use alias names to ensure that our safe haven is preserved.

As you know, I am Ozzie Tinman. It is nice to meet you and I look forward to seeing you in the Ozzie communities.

Find An Activity That Bolsters Self-Esteem: In your relationship, with the person with BPD, it is likely you were subjected to severe emotional abuse. The tactics that a person with BPD uses to break your spirit and self-esteem parallels the same tactics and manipulations that a violent physical abuser utilizes to keep their victim from leaving. See if these sound familiar: Isolation, Enforcing Trivia Demands, Depravation (sleep, food, things you need to function clearly), Threats, Occasional Indulgences (Hoovering), and Degradation & Criticism. I do not bring attention to this as a means of demonizing the person with BPD. Rather, it is important for you to realize that your emotional, and sometimes physical, scars run very deep. There is an enormous amount of damage that has been done to your self-esteem. Your self-esteem has been ripped to shreds and you have to start building yourself up again.

A good way to start developing your self-esteem is to participate in an activity that you enjoy and can observe immediately results. What activities did you sacrifice in the past as a means to meet the ever growing list of demands from your partner? Do you look back at your life and wonder why you did not continue to do something that you once loved? This is a great opportunity to begin again.

When I was given the advice to take on an activity I had no idea what to do. All these years I had focused so much on trying to make my wife happy, that when I actually had to think of something I enjoyed, I was at a loss. One night I sat down with a pencil and paper and just brainstormed everything I enjoyed doing in my past, all the way back to when I was a child. No matter how juvenile, it was on the list. After filling the paper, front and back, with everything from playing jacks to going on a cruise, I settled on the activity of going to the gym every other day. I enjoyed going and seeing people there, it would allow me to get physically healthy again, and maybe it is a "guy thing", but the immediate result of looking in the mirror and seeing actual muscle tone was very rewarding for me.

When I first started I set small attainable goals in regards to my exercise. I wanted the achievements to be fairly quick, but still a challenge. So instead of setting a goal to lose 50 pounds or bench pressing 300lbs, which would take a long time to achieve, I set small landmarks to meet. This allowed me to acknowledge my achievements on a regular basis and thus build my self-esteem, one brick at a time. Another great thing happened by taking on an activity. I was able to socialize, freely, without supervision. I had normal conversations with normal people, talked about everyday subjects rather than "safe subjects", and was able to just be myself. Let's see, "able to be oneself", add another brick. Two bricks became four, and four bricks became 8. Until one day I found that I had accumulated enough bricks that I could build a solid foundation of self-esteem. A foundation strong enough to withstand any abuse my wife could try to subject me to. What she had to say to, and about, me really didn't matter any longer. I felt good about myself. Like the Tin Man, I found my heart.

Hobbies: I view hobbies similar to an activity that bolsters self-esteem, but with a bit of a twist. Where self-esteem bolstering activities are chosen for a purpose of providing you a forum of achievement and building, hobbies I see as activities you participate in for the pure fun and enjoyment. There is no need to achieve anything, other than just being able to enjoy yourself. It doesn't matter if you do this hobby alone, with a friend, or with your children. The only requirement is that you do something you enjoy and have fun with.

Some of the things I chose to do didn't cost any money, require any effort, and focused completely on just allowing me to relax. Things like going to car shows or walking on the beach didn't require the spending of any money, but allowed me to enjoy the simple things that brought me and my children peace. I even began writing this book as an activity where I did something creative while I enjoyed the peace and quiet at the end of my day. All that matters is that you enjoy the activity that you choose to make your hobby. If going into the wild and snipe hunting with a potato sack strikes your fancy, by all means, do it.

You may even find that you enjoy your hobby so much that it evolves into an activity that bolsters your self-esteem. After going to various car shows, I decided that it would be fun to participate as an owner of a car in a show. Since my children were huge Herbie the Love Bug fans, I thought it was a perfect fit to restore a 1963 Volkswagen Herbie the Love Bug Replica. Now my children and I attend car shows and parades with our Love Bug, and have even won some People's Choice Awards along the way.

Take Care Of Your Body: A big part of allowing yourself to feel mentally good is to take physical care of yourself. If you do not take care of your body, you will be constantly worn down, ill, and unable to find the energy to devote to the mental demands you will have to face on your journey to Kansas.

By taking care of your body, I do not mean running the LA Marathon or devoting hours a day to developing the perfect body. You can take care of your body simply by eating a proper diet, getting enough sleep, and going for walks around the block.

Eating a proper diet is important because it is very difficult for your body to produce the energy that it needs to function property when you are not eating (or overeating), which many Ozzies tend to do as they neglect themselves. It is also difficult for your body to remain healthy and function properly if you are only eating fast food, which contains little nutritional value. Making your trip to Kansas is very stressful, and will require your thoughts to be clear and energy to be on reserve. Your plane can't take off from the runway if it is not filled with premium fuel. You need to properly prepare your body for this journey by giving it the fuel it needs and can use. Now don't get me wrong. I enjoy a good Big Mac and fries as much as the next person. But just be cautious not to make fast food your primary fuel...make it a treat. Your body will only give back to you what you put into it.

Getting enough sleep is essential. It is truly your pathway of a clear and rational mind. Without proper sleep you will be physically and mentally exhausted to the point that you will not be able to ward off the BPD's attempts to sabotage your journey to Kansas. Without proper sleep your thoughts will be muddied and you will be easily manipulated. Refer back to the section for bolstering self-esteem. One of the tactics a person with BPD will utilize to destroy your self-esteem, and control you, is sleep depravation. Depravation of sleep will make you susceptible to making bad decisions, as you will not have the clarity or energy to push back against things you know are not right. Like someone that is altered by alcohol, you lose your inhabitations and your self-control is lowered.

You will become an easy target for hoovering back to Oz.

Go to bed when you get tired, not at the bedtime that your partner sets for you. Then when you go to bed, actually go to sleep. I can recall many nights I laid in bed, festering and angry all night while my wife slept peacefully after she just finished raging at me. You need to allow yourself to relax and sleep. As you set stronger boundaries and build your self-esteem, this will become easier.

Finally, go for walks and exercise. Not only will this allow you to become physically stronger and build self-esteem, but it will also give you time to reflect about where you have been, where you are at, and where your journey is taking you. Some of the most dramatic light bulb moments that I have had on my journey have happened while I was running on a treadmill, with nothing else to do but think. During this quiet time let your mind wonder, explore what you want out of life, how you are going to get there, and if being involved in a BPD relationship will allow you to achieve your ambitions. As you explore your mind for answers, you will find that your walks will get farther and farther, and without even realizing it, you will get yourself in better and better physical condition.

Allow Yourself To Feel: When was the last time you felt angry? When was the last time you felt happy? When was the last time you felt anything…other than fear?

One of the huge side effects of being in an abusive relationship is that you begin to mute your emotions in an attempt to numb the daily pain that you are exposed to. You become a zombie walking from room to room and taking care of daily chores, as you function on autopilot. There is no happiness, sadness, anger, or joy. Just numbness. When you can experience emotions, it is likely fear and anxiety as your body goes into panic-mode in anticipation of a situation that you know will result in even more abuse.

When you are in a BPD relationship, this response is heightened even more as there is no predicting when and where this abuse is coming from. Will you get raged at for making dinner wrong? Will you get belittled for not taking the mail out of the box? What insignificant detail did you overlook that will result in today's emotional beating?

In order to start pulling yourself out of the emotional black hole that you are in, you are going to need to allow yourself to experience true emotions again. To do this you have to detach from the emotions of the person with BPD. Detachment is to emotionally separate yourself from another person so that they can be completely responsible for their own emotions and feelings. Refuse to allow them to make you feel as they do, constantly miserable. Instead, take control back of how you feel, as an individual. This means that you determine how you feel, what emotions you exhibit, and if your partner doesn't like it, that is just too bad.

Detaching from a person with BPD is not an easy task, as they are completely reliant upon you to define their identity. They live through you, your responses, and your emotions. If they feel bad about themselves, then they must make you feel bad about yourself as well (this is called projection). The person with BPD does not realize that you are an individual of your own, with your own feelings and emotions. They see you (and their children) as an extension of themselves, no different than an arm or a leg. Claiming your independence and taking ownership of your autonomy is equivalent to you chopping off one of their limbs, and they will fight to keep that from happening. You will have to be very assertive in refusing to allow the person with BPD to project upon and trying to control you. When you recognize that the person with BPD is trying to change your emotions and engage in behavior to manipulate how you are feeling, be very honest and clear with them. Make a direct statement such as, "No, that is how you feel. I will not allow you to make me carry that burden for you." As time goes by you will get better at recognizing when the person with BPD is trying to saddle you with their emotions and feelings, and you will develop your own effective responses to keep them from doing it.

Once you are able to construct a steel boundary to keep the person with BPD from giving you their emotions, you are able to free up the path to truly feeling your own emotions and feelings. Don't fight them back. If you feel like crying, then cry. If you want to smile, and be happy, then do it. It will be foreign at first, but that is ok. You are on your journey to the foreign land of Kansas.

You will find that when you first begin getting in touch with your emotions again, they will come flooding out like a dam has broken. You may cry with little provocation or get angry over little matters. Your happiness and joy may be overly optimistic. You will wonder if you are going crazy, or if you have lost control of your emotional state. Don't panic. Think of your emotions like a wire coil. For years the person with BPD has been pulling it, distorting it, causing it to accumulate a great amount of tension. What happens when you let go of that wire coil and all the tension that has built up? It springs back wildly, jumping every which way, until finally it falls into a natural motion, and settles in equilibrium. Your emotions will have the same reaction, and jump all over, until they find a natural and healthy balance.

Seek Individual Therapy: A personal therapist is a fantastic resource that many Ozzies overlook during their journey. Due to the misconceptions of society in general, many Ozzies believe that going to a therapist for assistance and guidance proves that they themselves are not mentally healthy. Nothing could be farther from the truth.

Many healthy people use the assistance of a therapist as a means of keeping their thoughts centered, focus on goals, and to help deal with the many changes happening in their lives. During your journey you are going to experience great highs, and deep lows, confusion, anxiety, fear, anger, and a wide range of other emotions that you may not be able to interpret on your own. Sharing these emotions with a therapist may help you determine where they are coming from, what they mean to you, and proper ways to respond to the signs your body is giving to you. To have emotions and feelings is human. Therapists specialize in helping your body and mind speak to one another so that these feelings, and emotions, can be used in a positive manner. This can only be healthy. Why would you deny yourself something that can only benefit you? To deny help when it is needed, and available, would truly be the act of a mentally unhealthy person.

The decision to seek a personal therapist is one that you must make based on your own needs and comfort. However, if you do seek therapy, it is vitally important that you choose a therapist or psychiatrist with experience in treating clients with Borderline Personality Disorder and their family members. You are going to need a therapist that is familiar with the extreme behaviors that a person with BPD exhibits, as well as the possible destruction of other lives that behavior can result in. To determine if a therapist is qualified to meet your treatment needs ask them:

What specialized training have you had for treating clients with BPD and their families?

What is your understanding of BPD, the behaviors exhibited, and its effects on family members?

Do you believe that BPD is curable? To your understanding what is the treatment period of a client with BPD?

Are you familiar with the various treatment methods for BPD and which do you utilize?

What percentage of your clients are diagnosed with BPD and/or are family members?

Any therapist that has experience and expertise in treating clients with BPD should have no problem answering any of these questions. Nor should they feel intimidated by you asking for their treatment credentials, beliefs and methods. If you come across a therapist that can't give you clear answers to these questions, or tries to give obviously false answers (i.e. telling you they can cure a person with BPD in 6 months) then look for another therapist that has legitimate experience in addressing your treatment needs. There is nothing wrong with shopping around for a therapist that you are comfortable with.

Strength Reminders And Mementos: The trip to Kansas is not a smooth flight. It is filled with a lot of turbulence, dips, rises, and will feel as though you are on a roller coaster ride at times. During parts of your journey you will hit very low points where you feel like you can't go on. You will think that returning to Oz is the easiest way out, and you will actually consider standing up in the aisle and yelling, "Ozzie Tinman! Turn this plane around." Of course I will refuse to do so, and tell you if you want to get off the plane then that is your choice, and that there are plenty of parachutes available. After all, I do not want to see you go back to Oz, but you have to make up your own mind and be responsible for your own decisions (sound familiar?).

To help yourself get through some of these low periods, I have found that Strength Reminders and Mementos can do wonders to keep you moving forward. A strength reminder or memento is a physical object that you keep with you that reminds you where you have been, where you are now, and where you are going. Some Ozzies carry inspiring poems, some have a special piece of jewelry, some have a token or a coin, some write themselves letters. The object chosen is usually very personal and meaningful to the Ozzie that carries it.

On my journey to Kansas I have used two strength reminders and mementos. The first was the book "Stop Walking On Eggshells", by Paul Mason and Randi Kreger. This book inspired and assisted me so much in working through my pain that I gave it a center spot on my worktable in my office. There is not a day that I don't walk by my office, see it sitting there, and remind myself just how far I have come on my journey. When I first found myself in Oz, I was perhaps one of the most pitiful and weak Ozzies out there. But with the help from this book, as well as other support systems and self-determination, I was able to gain control of my life.

The next strength reminder and memento that I have been using since November 15, 2004, is a Lance Armstrong Cancer Research bracelet. It is a simple yellow rubber bracelet with the phrase "LIVE STRONG" imprinted into it. November 15, 2004, is the day I left my wife and decided to seek a divorce.

On that day one of my co-workers came into my office, saw that I was not my normal self, and asked if I was okay. I told her that I had left my wife that morning and that I would be seeking a divorce. She took the bracelet off her wrist, gave it to me, gave

me a kiss on the cheek and said, "Steve, Live
Strong." My eyes welled up with tears, and I
thanked her for the bracelet. I immediately put it on
my wrist and have worn it ever since. It is a
reminder to me of the wonderful support from
friends and family that I have received during my
journey. And the imprinted phrase on the bracelet,
"**LIVE STRONG**", seems to say it all.

Chapter 6

Borderline Defense Mechanisms And Control Tactics

Chapter 6

Borderline Defense Mechanisms And Control Tactics

When a person with BPD feels threatened by abandonment, feels negative about themselves, or that their disorder will be exposed, they will go into panic-mode to protect themselves. As a result of feeling that they must protect themselves, the person with BPD has an arsenal of internal defense mechanisms and control tactics to use as a means of protecting against the person they view as the threat. Many times their belief that they are about to be abandoned or exposed is only a distortion of their own thoughts. As such, it appears to the Ozzie that the behavior is an unprovoked offensive attack. However, it is important to understand that to the person with BPD, their displayed aggression is a response to their fear, and intended to be defensive as a means of protecting their self-image.

A Defense Mechanism is a subconscious response intended to protect a person from establishing a negative self-image and to minimize anxiety. Even mentally healthy people use defense mechanisms every day of their lives in a healthy manner. They help us deal with setbacks and negative situations in a way that we do not internalize the negative incident as a means of defining our "self" as bad. However, as mentally healthy individuals with a concrete sense of right and wrong, we understand there are many shades of gray in between. We are able to comprehend that if something negative happens, it does not result in our "self" being all bad. We understand that the negative situation likely falls in the gray area to some degree, and that the one incident does not define our entire reality or identity. There is a remedy, life goes on, and we are still inherently a good person.

On the other hand, the person with BPD does not have the ability to see gray areas. Their perception of the world is "all or nothing", and one negative incident results in them believing that they are all bad. So their defense mechanisms respond at an unhealthy level because their reactions are so exaggerated and inappropriate for the situation they believe they are facing. Their overreaction negatively affects their ability to function interpersonally and sometimes societally.

It is important for Ozzies to understand the defense mechanisms and control tactics that a person with BPD utilizes and why they use them. Without understanding why a person with BPD responds how they do, the Ozzie will attempt to use rationale and logic to determine how to respond to the situation. This will not work. Remember that the person with BPD is responding with pure emotion, which is the opposite of rationale and logic. So if you are trying to make logical sense of their behavior, you and the person with BPD will be speaking two different languages. Chances are your loved one will think you are being condescending to them, and the situation will become more elevated.

Let's go over some of the more common defense mechanisms and control tactics a person with BPD utilizes, and common motives for their use.

Defense Mechanisms

Acting Out: Acting out is when an individual deals with their emotions or stressors through exaggerated actions, rather than reflections of their feelings. This is where the person with BPD will Rage or attempt suicide.

A person with BPD lives through their emotions. Their emotions define their physical reality and are their means of expression. Their emotions come in tidal waves and the person finds themselves unable to conceal or express this emotion in an appropriate manner. As a result, the person with BPD does not just get upset, they become irate. They do not just get sad, they become clinically depressed.

Since the display of emotion in exaggerated fashion is their means of expressing themselves, you get behaviors like Rages due to fear, anxiety or anger. You get verbal attacks because the person with BPD goes into a panic and must express verbally what they are feeling at that moment. Since their feelings overwhelm them, they express it in a way that is also overwhelming to you.

Acting out is essentially expressing one's emotions through physical actions, in an inappropriate and harmful manner. When dealing with a person who is acting out, look at the actions as an emotion. Think to yourself, "what emotion is tied to this behavior." For example, if the person is cutting themselves, perhaps they are saying, "I am bad and deserve to feel pain", or "I do not feel real. I need to feel pain so I know I am real."

Denial: Denial is the failure to recognize obvious implications or consequences of an act or situation. People with BPD live in denial as they constantly refuse to acknowledge their behaviors are harmful to those around them. They further refuse to acknowledge that their behaviors are the root of many of their friends and family leaving the relationship after being hurt. Rather, they see nothing wrong with their negative behaviors and feel entitled to do anything they please without consequence.

The person's failure to recognize that consequences are attached to their actions results in them engaging in such abusive behaviors as raging, belittling, distortion campaigns, and constant accusations. If the Ozzie can no longer tolerate the abuse, the person with BPD will point the finger at the Ozzie and claim the Ozzie abandoned them, without recognizing the root cause that drove the Ozzie away.

In my case my wife accused me of molesting our children and insisted that I take a lie detector to show I was not doing the horrible things she alleged. After I took and passed the test, I told my wife what a huge breach of trust she committed by accusing me of such things, and that it would take a long time for me to forgive her. My wife's response was, "Get over it and move on. That is just how I felt and I should be able to say anything I want. After all, if I did not accuse you then I would have been a bad mother because I 'knew' something was not right." Later, after she again accused me, for the second time and I left, I told her that I would be divorcing her as a result of her continued allegations. My wife told me to, "Stop being dramatic. It is not that bad." She was unable to connect the severity of her accusations with the trauma that resulted, and ultimately the justifiable consequences of me leaving. To this day she still denies that her accusations were an appropriate reason for leaving the marriage.

So why is denial such a huge part of the BPD condition? Well, to admit that they are wrong, their actions are hurtful, or that they are directly responsible for consequences, is to acknowledge that they are evil people, in their own minds. Denial keeps the person with BPD from facing the truth that they have hurt people, have caused people to abandon them, and that they are responsible for many of their own problems. To avoid this responsibility, their brain does a switch-a-roo to tell them that their actions are in fact the correct thing to do. It is the other people that are wrong, hurtful, and responsible for what happened.

Dissociation: Dissociation is when the person with BPD will no longer be responding to the situation, circumstances, or environment before them. Rather, their emotional responses and anger are being triggered and caused by a past traumatic event that causes them great pain. They may exhibit strange behaviors or responses that make no sense to the Ozzie, because the Ozzie is trying to address the current crisis, not the past emotional issues of the person with BPD. During episodes of dissociation, it is likely the person with BPD will have a form of amnesia where they will later not remember the behavior they engaged in or hurtful things they said. To the person with BPD, the incident never happened, and there will be no convincing them otherwise. If you try to speak to them later about their behavior, chances are you will get a blank stare with denials that the incident ever happened. Further, the person with BPD may actually accuse you of being the person that engaged in the negative behaviors, as they cast you as the villain when their brain attempts to reconstruct and make sense of the incident.

Dissociation occurs because the past emotion that is being triggered is so painful that the person with BPD is not able to face the pain on a conscious level. Although something in the present triggered the emotional response, once dissociation takes hold, the expression is no longer about what the current trigger is. The response is about their past pain, and the current incident gets stored or compartmentalized in the subconscious with the painful emotions of the past. Once the crisis is gone, so are the person's memories of the incident. However, it is common for the person with BPD to resort back to this information when they dissociate again in the future.

You need to remind yourself that your loved one's dissociation has nothing to do with you. It is about their emotional pain and scars from their past and childhood. Be mindful that they are in real pain, and even though they may be misplacing their aggression towards you, if it is safe to do so maintain your empathy for their pain.

Projection: Your loved one is raging. They are yelling at you, calling you names, and is obviously angry. They then look at you and says, "You are so hostile towards me! Why do you do this to me?" You are confused because you did not do anything to indicate you were hostile, nor were you showing any anger towards them. What your loved one did was project her feelings onto you. This is called Projection. Projection is attributing one's thoughts or impulses to another person, and normally pertains to unacceptable or undesirable behaviors.

A person with BPD projects their actions, thoughts, and emotions onto the Ozzie as a means of not having to own, or be responsible, for their negative thoughts and behaviors. The behaviors that they engage in are so harmful and destructive that taking ownership for them could result in their acknowledgement that they are doing something inappropriate and wrong. This acknowledgment could result in them seeing themselves as all bad (splitting). The person with BPD attributes those negative thoughts and behaviors onto someone else to be responsible for them.

Many Ozzies are accused of having affairs, only to find out that the person with BPD is having an affair. The Ozzie may be accused of being controlling, when the person with BPD is dictating every aspect of their relationship and life. The person with BPD may tell the Ozzie that they are a terrible parent, when really the person with BPD believes that they themselves are a bad parent.

When a person with BPD accuses you of something that makes absolutely no sense, then there is a good chance they are projecting. However, this is not the rule all of the time, as some people with BPD also suffer from paranoia and delusions, which could also be a factor in their accusations. The rule of thumb is if a person with BPD is telling you how

YOU FEEL, then it is likely projections. Here are some examples of interpreting projection:

"You hate me" = "I don't know why you like me. I don't even like myself."

"You are always angry at me." = "I am always angry and don't know why."

"You are so controlling." = "I feel like I have no control over myself."

"Kindness is your weapon. You kill me with kindness." = "I don't deserve to be treated with kindness."

Where projection gets tricky is when the person with BPD is accusing you of doing some physical action rather than attributing a feeling. It is common for a person with BPD to accuse their spouse of having affairs, taking drugs, or other physical acts. The big question, is this projection? Unfortunately, there is no clear answer. Some Ozzies find that it is projection, and that their partners are engaged in those behaviors. Some people with BPD are just the accusatory type and they are not projecting. So do not immediately jump to the conclusion that every false accusation is a projection. That is not always the case. But do raise an eyebrow of caution. My wife's accusations against me of molesting our children were not a

projection. Rather, they were just manifestations of
her paranoia and delusions.

Projective Identification: This is the close cousin
to projection. Where Projection is the person with
BPD attributing emotions or behaviors to you that
you do not display, Projective Identification is when
the person with BPD successfully gets you to
display the emotion or behavior, and you take them
as your own.

In this situation, the person with BPD may say to
you, "Why are you so mad, you are always mad at
me." You do not start off with this emotion, but as a
result of their accusations, you do get mad and
respond, "you're damn right I am mad!" You just
identified with their projection, and accepted that as
your own emotion.

Those with BPD are masters at this. They are very
savvy at creating their own reality to confirm to
what their perceptions are. People with BPD can be
so effective at this that they have been known to
manipulate therapists into accepting and identifying
with their projections. Where this often comes up is
during couple's therapy sessions where the person
with BPD will idolize the therapist. They will place
the therapist on a pedestal and cast them as their
protector by portraying a victim. When the Ozzie
comes to the session, the therapist will protect the
person with BPD, thus making the Ozzie feel
ganged up on. If you begin to feel that this is

happening in your couple's session, you may want to schedule an individual session with the therapist and express your concerns.

What purpose would this serve for the person with BPD? It validates their view of "reality." It proves to them that they are not crazy. They are not paranoid or delusional, since you just confirmed their perception. You were exactly what you were accused of being. In the situation with the therapist, again it validates their perceptions. By the therapist openly protecting the person with BPD, it confirms that they are the victim in the dynamic. After all, even the therapist recognizes that they are the victim, which make you the bad guy.

Splitting: A person with BPD sees the world in black and white. Things and people are either all good or all evil, completely right or completely wrong, all black or all white. Due to this highly structured and rigid process of thinking, the person with BPD does not realize that there are vast areas of gray in which most of reality exists. As a result, the person with BPD views the people in their life in extremes of good and evil.

The process in which a person with BPD classifies another person as All Good or All Evil is called "Splitting." During a period when an Ozzie is "split white", the person with BPD will idolize them and seek to emulate their behaviors. The Ozzie will be placed high on a pedestal and given much praise.

When split white the person with BPD will try to draw the Ozzie emotionally closer. On the other side of the coin is the Ozzie being split black. This will result in the person with BPD devaluing the Ozzie and finding faults with virtually everything about them. Their behaviors, their character, their motives, will all be brought into question, with the person with BPD being the judge and jury. During this time, the person with BPD will push the Ozzie away, far away.

Splitting of the Ozzie can occur at any time and for any reason. The Ozzie does not have to do anything to be split either way. Nor can the they do anything to avoid being split. Rather, the person with BPD will split the Ozzie according to their fear and perceptions of their reality. There are times when the Ozzie's actions will cause a split, when those actions cause the person with BPD to fear they are about to be abandoned.

The purpose of splitting is to validate the thought process and perception of the person with BPD. When the Ozzie does something that is perceived as harmful or threatening, the person with BPD must justify to themselves that it is okay to think badly of the Ozzie. The person with BPD will hone in on all of the Ozzie's faults to validate to themselves, "yeah, this is really a bad person, and there is nothing redeeming about them." The person with BPD will magnify faults and elaborate so greatly that their perceptions will no longer reflect actual reality. However, to the person with BPD, their perceptions are very real.

It is important for the Ozzie to not bask in the sun when they are being split white. Your instincts are to enjoy the time when the person with BPD is thinking highly of you; however, you must keep in mind that accepting idolization will have serious consequences later when you are split back black. Many times when you are being split white to black, the severity of the negative split will be in proportion to the level at which you were idolized. If you are placed high on the pedestal, then when you fall it will be a very long way down.

When an Ozzie is being split white, correct the false perception. If you are not deserving of the high praise, then politely thank the person with BPD for the compliment, but then make a reality statement that what you did was not as fantastic as is being expressed. By doing so, and keeping the person's perceptions of you more grounded, you may avoid the severity of your future return to being split black.

In regards to splitting, another concern to consider is for those with children. It is common for a parent with BPD to split their children, where one will be split black and one will be split white. One will be the Golden Child, and one will be the troubled child. This is how a parent with BPD will classify their children, and it will play a drastic role in how they parent each child. This dynamic will likely have a negative impact on the children as the children will be constantly pitted against each other, creating an environment saturated with resentment and negative feelings. With little provocation, the parent with BPD will flip the splitting of their children, and roles will be reversed. Such instability leads to a lot of confusion for the children and does not allow them to find safety within their home environment.

Control Tactics

Isolation: At one time many Ozzies were fairly social personalities. However, as their relationship with the person with BPD continued they found that they socialized less, created distance from friends, and felt as though they lost contact with their extended family. This is not by accident. It is very common for the person with BPD to insist that all of the Ozzie's attention be focused on them at all times. It is also very common for the person with BPD to drive wedges between Ozzies and their friends and family as a means of keeping the Ozzie from socializing. These wedges may come in the form of causing conflicts, making false allegations, or constantly finding fault. The end result is that the Ozzie is alone, friendless, and without any family support.

The person with BPD isolates the Ozzie from society for two main reasons. First, the Ozzie has insight into the person with BPD, and their odd and irrational behaviors. The more they socialize outside of supervision, the more likely they will reveal the secrets of what goes on behind the closed doors of their home. Second is the fear of abandonment. If the Ozzie has no one in their life other than the person with BPD, then they will be less likely to leave. After all, nobody wants to be alone. So the Ozzie is placed in a situation where they must decide, live alone in solitude or tolerate the abuse. Since part of codependency is being fearful of being alone, many Ozzies choose to stay and tolerate the abuse rather than leaving and taking the risk of being alone.

Self-Fulfilling Prophecies: How often has your loved one accused you of something or claimed that something terrible was going to happen, only to be the very person that caused the result? People with BPD are notorious for "predicting" a negative future event, just to turn around and create the situation in which the prediction occurs. This is a self-fulfilling prophecy.

A common self-fulfilling prophecy that a person with BPD will make is that someone specific will abandon them. They may claim that you, the Ozzie, secretly hates them and will eventually leave. You try to reassure them that you love them and have no intent to leave. Then your loved one will begin to engage in hateful, and sometimes harmful, behavior directed at you. They may become so elevated in their hostility that you have no choice but to leave for your own safety. As you walk out of the door, the person with BPD will say, "I always knew you would leave me."

This is exactly what my wife did. For a year she accused me of having a plan to leave and that I was just waiting for her to do something wrong so that I could abandon her. Even after she accused me of molesting our children the first time, claimed I was a master hypnotist and controlling her, raged at me nightly, verbally and emotionally abused me, and threatened to call the police to arrest me on multiple occasions, I stayed with her. Then, finally after she accused me of molesting our children for the second time, I told her I could not tolerate her abuse any longer and was leaving the marriage. She again claimed that I had a plan to leave her, and that she had been right all along.

The purpose of making self-fulfilling prophecies is so they can validate their thinking and perception of the world around them. They need to prove to themselves that they are not crazy and do think rationally. What better way to do this than to be able to know exactly what the outcome of their situation is going to be? It allows the person with BPD to think that they do have a grasp on reality. It allow them to validate that they are not the crazy one in the relationship. After all, a crazy person would not be able to rationalize what the future outcome will be. What the person with BPD does not realize is that they are not predicting the future; they are creating situations that will intentionally cause the predicted outcome.

Catch 22: You are damned if you do, and you are damned if you don't. No matter what you answer or what you do, you are always wrong. This is the life of an Ozzie, as their existence is filled with Catch 22 situations in which there is no correct outcome. The person with BPD can always find something that should have been different or better.

A classic situation where the Ozzie finds himself in a Catch 22 is by trying to get emotionally close with the person with BPD. If the Ozzie tries to get too close they are harshly rejected because the person with BPD fears intimacy. If the Ozzie backs away from the person, then they are accused of being cold and distant. There is no solution since either way the person with BPD will be triggered and blame the Ozzie.

Another common Catch 22 is when the person with BPD has concluded that the Ozzie has done something wrong. They will go to the Ozzie and confront them. The Ozzie is placed in the situation where if they admits the behavior the person with BPD will attack them as an evil person and untrustworthy. If the Ozzie denies the accusation, the person will call them a liar and insist they are being dishonest.

People with BPD engage in this behavior when they are in the process of splitting the Ozzie black. They constantly set up situations where, no matter how the Ozzie responds, they are presented in a negative light. This validates the person's decision to split the Ozzie black since time and time again the person with BPD judges them to be a "bad person." Then viola, the splitting of the Ozzie is complete.

Distortion Campaigns: When the person with BPD perceives that the Ozzie has or will abandon them, this is likely to result in them immediately engaging in a distortion campaign against the Ozzie. A distortion campaign is when the person with BPD goes to friends and family, and unjustly attacks the character of the Ozzie. The distortion arises when the person with BPD begins to use lies and distorts the truth as a means of smearing the Ozzie. During this period the person with BPD will claim the Ozzie engaged in harmful acts against them that never occurred. They will tell your friends and family that you did horrible things to them, and may even make false criminal allegations against you. A distortion campaign is a panicked response to "prove" that you are the reason that the relationship ended, and they were merely the innocent victim in the matter.

After I left my wife and told her I would be seeking a divorce, she went on a massive distortion campaign against me. She called all of the people we knew and told them that I was a horrible tyrant in our home and emotionally abused her and our children. She told her family that I controlled their every move, and that I sabotaged her relationship between her, her father, and her sister. She even called my own mother to attempt to persuade her that I unjustly left the marriage, and that I was not doing what was best for our children. For good measure she told all the people we knew that I had a plan all along to make her look crazy, divorce her, and steal the children from her. Despite the absurdity of her claims, some of the people believed her. However, she was sure to leave out all of her destructive behaviors over the years and the false molestation accusations she made against me.

The purpose of engaging in a distortion campaign is largely to gain false sympathy and support, as the person with BPD portrays themselves as the victim. The people that believe them validate their belief that you are a bad person, and therefore deserved to be split black. The person with BPD now has an arsenal of supporters that constantly protect and validate their thoughts. In their mind, they must be in the right and justified in their negative behavior that they direct towards you.

The person with BPD can use a distortion campaign as a source of control a couple of different ways. If the Ozzie is very self-conscious about their image, then the distortion campaign may be a means of hoovering them back into the relationship. The Ozzie may become so worried that their reputation may be harmed that they may decide to return to the relationship to stop the damage from occurring. Another way that distortion campaign empowers the person with BPD is through isolation. By discrediting the Ozzie and causing people to think poorly of them, the Ozzie may find themselves alone and without support. They may also find themselves constantly on the defense as they try to combat the false claims.

I have found that the best result to a distortion campaign is no response. No matter what you say or do, the person with BPD is going to talk poorly about you. There is nothing you can do about it. At times friends and family may come to you and tell you what the person with BPD has said about you. I would usually thank them for their concern, and tell them, "I have no idea why she would say such a thing, but you should know me well enough to make your own judgement." Then leave it up to the person to decide for themselves. Taking the high road in this situation has always paid off for me in the end. You will feel better about yourself for not mudslinging, and eventually the lies and distortions will reveal themselves as misinformation.

Redefining Reality: How often has the person with BPD told you something that made absolutely no sense or that you knew was completely false? However, when they made the statement to you they seemed to actually believe what they were saying. This is because the mind of a person with BPD will redefine reality and twist it to fit what they want it to be, rather than what is accurate. Many times they will use their warped sense of reality to try to justify their actions or get you to change yours.

I often experienced this with my wife when she was upset because I would refuse to give into a request of hers. She would make claims that her "friends" (she never specified which ones) would come to her and tell her I should be doing what she requested. If that didn't work, then she would claim her therapist agreed with her on the subject and confirmed I was being unreasonable. An example of this might have gone as such: "Even (therapist), a trained professional, agrees that I should be the person that says prayers with the kids every night."

On one occasion I confronted her therapist about validating beliefs that were obviously harmful, based on her claims of his support. The therapist denied supporting her claims as she indicated and only acknowledged that it came up in a session and he listened to her. In this instance she redefined her reality to reflect that his mere listening to her beliefs, without expressing disagreement, was a form of validation. She then, in turn, attempted to use his silence as "support" as a basis for argument to get what she was requesting.

A person with BPD may also redefine reality as a means of avoiding responsibility for their actions. By redefining an incident they can attribute the negative behavior to someone else (projection), deny that the behaviors ever happened, or create additional circumstances that will justify the negative behavior.

The Ozzie must remember to take their "proof" with a grain of salt, unless they have actual hard facts to present. Accepting their word at face value may result in you having a very inaccurate perception of what the situation truly is. You could act in a manner that is not warranted, just as I did when I confronted my wife's therapist. Always keep in mind that a person with BPD sees reality and situations as they want to see them, not as they truly are.

Chapter 7

Ozzie Stinkin' Thinkin'

Chapter 7

Ozzie Stinkin' Thinkin'

During your journey to Kansas you will come to realize that much of your thinking is distorted. As you come to realize this, your brain will scramble to make sense of the world and you will begin to question many things about your perceptions. This is part of the healing process. Allow yourself to explore and dissect your thoughts, and the world, so that you can begin to draw a distinct line between what is real and what is illusion.

Exploring your reality and coming to understand that much of the world you lived in was distorted will not be an easy task. It is scary, and your mind will strive feverishly to try to make rational sense about what has happened to you in your relationship. You will feel exhausted trying to process your experiences. The more you try to make sense of the person with BPD, the more you will be left confused and without answers. Borderline Personality Disorder is truly an insane disorder with little rhyme or reason. Allowing it to consume your thoughts could in turn drive you crazy. This is why it is important for the Ozzie to remain focused on their own issues and matters that they have control over.

In trying to determine what is real and what is imaginary, your mind will question your beliefs. You will begin to question yourself as a person, question others in your life, and try to grasp every last straw to find hope that the person with BPD will miraculously get better. After all, you still love this person and to lose hope is to lose the person you love. Ozzies begin to doubt themselves, others, and want so badly to retain hope. It is common for the Ozzie to develop unhealthy thoughts in their desperate attempt to rationalize staying with the person with BPD.

When an Ozzie begins to express or act on these unhealthy thoughts, the Ozzie community refers to this as Stinkin' Thinkin', Oz Thinking, or Non-Sense. This is one of the huge benefits of being involved in support groups. Fellow Ozzies are very intuitive and vocal about when they recognize that another person in the group has fallen into this pattern of thinking. It is vital that an Ozzie recognizes when they are engaging in Stinkin' Thinkin', otherwise they will likely suffer a hard fall back into Oz.

In this chapter we will review some of the common subjects and questions that come up when an Ozzie engages in Stinkin' Thinkin'.

Everyone Has BPD!: After years of abuse, pain, and being blamed for absolutely everything, you have finally come to the point where you can look at your situation and say, "I didn't cause my loved one's behaviors." It is a substantial stride in your recovery and a huge burden that you have been relieved of. For many years you were blind to the abuse, thought you were the problem, and accepted all of the blame. However, now you understand that there is a diagnosis that explains the chaos, turmoil, and hurt in your life.

After finding out that your loved one has BPD, you go out and research the disorder. You gain a firm understanding of the nine criteria and you can pinpoint exactly how your loved one fits at least five of them. But guess what else you start doing? You start assessing everyone else in your life as well. You start thinking of other difficult people in your life, "Hmm, perhaps Aunt Millie has BPD too." You think about it and according to your assessment she does fit at least five of the nine criteria. Then you assess Grandma, Uncle Jim, the neighbor, and just for good measure the dog that keeps getting into your trash. They all have BPD too! You are surrounded by people (and dogs) who have Borderline Personality Disorder!

Ozzies fall into this trap because after they realize that there is a label to describe the behavior of their love one, Ozzies become hyper-sensitive to the abusive behaviors and traits. However, what the

Ozzie fails to understand is that every person on Earth possesses the traits listed in the analysis of Borderline Personality Disorder. Many of these traits are just part of being human. Some of these "borderline traits" can be utilized in a positive and productive manner by a person that is mentally healthy. What the Ozzie will do is begin dissecting the difficult people in their lives and remember sporadic incidents where the person got angry, or yelled, or utilized a "borderline behavior" as a means of coping with stress, failing to realize that these incidents were sporadic, and not a regular occurrence. The Ozzie will match five sporadic events, and BINGO, the Ozzie is convinced that the person has BPD.

It is important for Ozzies to remember that only approximately 2% of the population actually meet the criteria for Borderline Personality Disorder. To meet the criteria, the behaviors have to be so extreme that they negatively impact the person's ability to have a healthy relationship and function in interpersonal relationships. If you are looking around and are convinced that 60% of the people around you have BPD, then chances are you are overgeneralizing the traits to everyone in your life. Remember that these traits must be pervasive in the person's personality, and sporadic occurrences do not qualify as "pervasive."

Maybe I Am Crazy Or Have BPD: At some point during your journey to Kansas, you will ask yourself, "Maybe I am the crazy one. Maybe I am the person with BPD." You will become worried that perhaps you are covertly the person diagnosed with BPD rather than your loved one. Perhaps the therapist is withholding the diagnosis from you because you are the person with the fragile ego that they don't want to trigger.

Here is the simple truth, if you are expressing concern that you are crazy, or have BPD, than chances are that you are neither. As a rule of thumb, crazy people do not question their sanity, and people with BPD do not assume they have the disorder. Rather, when they begin to suspect that something is not right in their thought process, their defense mechanisms go into full overdrive and they begin projecting and blaming. For a person with BPD to admit that they have the disorder and are flawed, it usually takes years of intensive therapy, a lot of hard work, and serious soul searching. Not to mention, virtually a loss of all their interpersonal relationships, including friends, family, spouses, children, etc. They pretty much have to hit rock bottom before any progress is made, and they have nowhere else to point their finger other than at themselves. A person with BPD does not just wake up one day and think, "you know, I think I have BPD." Due to the nature of this disorder, and the intense fear of the person admitting that they are flawed, their defense mechanisms keep them from seeing what is obvious to those closest to them, that they are mentally ill. The person with BPD will perceive that they are perfectly normal, and it is everyone else that are wrong and mentally ill.

If you have the ability to question the possibility that you have BPD, then chances are that you do not.

Giving Is Bad: You have been hurt. You have been taken advantage of. And why did this happen? One reason is because you were willing to give so much of yourself to a relationship that it became unhealthy. Your loved one took advantage of your willingness to give. They took and took from you, until you literally gave everything you had, and lost yourself.

After your loved one's disorder was exposed, you found out that one of the requirements of making yourself better was to start caring for yourself. You also learned that you had to distance yourself emotionally, and had to stop giving to the person with BPD if you were going to make advancements in your recovery. During this process many Ozzies develop a false belief that giving emotionally to another person is bad. It exposes you emotionally and makes you vulnerable to being hurt again. Your thought process interprets your pain to convince you that you shouldn't give to another person, and this will protect you from being hurt again in the future.

This may work temporarily during your early recovery because one of the first steps you must take is to direct your efforts towards caring for yourself. However, after you get yourself centered and moving in a healthy direction, where you are meeting many of your own needs, there will come a time when cutting yourself off emotionally from the world will only lead to your own self-isolation.

As human beings we have a need to interact socially, to be in relationships, and to give and take in a healthy relationship. If this were not the case then we might as well find a cave, light a fire, and stay there alone. There are needs that we have that we personally can't meet on our own, such as intimacy. Developing a relationship that fosters intimacy requires that both partners give and take emotionally from one another, without losing one's individuality.

If an Ozzie stays in the frame of mind that giving emotionally is bad, then they will never be able to develop the intimate relationships that they crave and need. The Ozzie will be too busy defending and protecting themselves from people getting too close to them, and will end up pushing everyone away. This is very similar to what the person with BPD does, and why they are not able to have a truly intimate relationship.

The Ozzie must understand that distancing themselves emotionally from the person with BPD was only a step to accommodate their recovery, and not a lesson for maintaining a relationship. It was to teach and develop that personal boundaries are essential, and to understand that bulldozing over another person's boundaries are not part of a healthy relationship. When the lessons are learned from these necessary steps, then the Ozzie can begin to learn to develop healthy relationships. To do this, they will have to learn to give, and take, emotionally. They will have to break the cycle of allowing an emotional vampire to drain them, where they serve as a one-way spicket allowing the person with BPD to sucks them emotionally dry. The Ozzie must learn that in a healthy relationship that both parties give and take, drawing from and re-filling each other's emotional gas tanks to ensure they both remain emotionally fulfilled.

Becoming Fixated On BPD: What was the first thing you did when you found out that your loved one's behavior had a name? What did you do when you found out it was called Borderline Personality Disorder? If you were anything like me, and many other Ozzies, you ran out and looked up as much information as you could find. You wanted to understand what you were dealing with and how you could "assist" the person you care about. As you have been reading, there is very little you can do to assist their recovery. Just like your journey to Kansas is about your own self-discovery, they too are on their own journey, and you must respect that the two journeys are independent. You can't make their journey for them, and they can't make yours.

During the process of learning about BPD many Ozzies will find themselves obsessing about the disorder. It will consume their thoughts day and night as they try to figure out what they can do to "fix" the situation. Of course this is a human response, because in general people want solutions to problems. Most issues in life have a solution that will fix the situation. However, what Ozzies fail to realize is that this disorder is not about them. Yes, they have been swept up in the tornado, but at the core of this situation is the person with BPD, who is the only person that can address their disorder. Ozzies will search high and low, looking for a solution what will miraculously bring their life back into balance. In time they discover that they are so engulfed in seeking so much information about BPD that every other aspect of their life begins to suffer.

I went through a period of about three months of obsessing about this disorder. I spend all my time, at home and at work, sending emails to the support group, looking up BPD websites, and trying to find every shred of information available. If there was a silver bullet out there to "fix" my wife, I was going to find it. Looking back, I have no idea how I kept my employment during this time because I simply was not working. Perhaps the only thing that saved my job was that I went to my Director and informed

her of my situation at home, and perhaps she felt
sorry for me. But due to my obsessing, my work
habits went down the drain, in law school I went
from A's and B's to barely maintaining C's, and
there was a period when I was being a bad father
because I wasn't available emotionally to my
children. All because I allowed my wife's disorder
to consume me and dictate my life. So although I
may have escaped by wife physically, emotionally I
was still firmly in Oz.

There is no doubt that educating yourself and
gaining insight as to how a BPD relationship affects
you and your recovery is paramount. You must
remind yourself that there is a definite line where
seeking information becomes consuming and has a
negative impact upon your life. If you find that the
time you spend seeking answers and information
about BPD is negatively affecting other important
aspects of your life, then it's time to take a break.
That's where your line is. Reassess where your
focus is, and direct it towards elements of your life
that will encourage moving forward in a positive
direction.

If you find that you have a need to seek information
about BPD, and how it affects you, then perhaps set
some rules for yourself to follow. Limit your time
dedicated to BPD research to work breaks or an
hour before bedtime. The important thing is that
you do not allow this search for information, or
participation in groups, to interfere with what

normal life you do have. By allowing BPD to consume your free time, you have just given up what little bit of normalcy you do have by burying yourself even deeper into this disorder. Remind yourself that the goal in this journey is to escape from Oz, not to entrench yourself even deeper.

False Hope For The Person With BPD: Ozzies tend to be overly optimistic and hopeful about the people they care about. Built into our giving nature is a belief in the good of those around us and that things always work out for the best. We are constantly looking for that silver lining in the dark cloud, even if we have to squint our eyes really hard…we know it is there, somewhere.

In many situations this hopefulness serves us well and can be a great attribute. We are often the person that serves as the motivating influence in a group when people are ready to give up, and we are the remaining voice saying, "give it one more try." However, in the Ozzie and BPD relationship, this hopefulness can make us blind to the fact that Borderline Personality Disorder is a lifelong condition. Even with an unusually motivated person that makes huge treatment efforts, receives appropriate therapy, and is willing to make changes, the truth is that currently there is no cure for BPD. People with BPD that make a huge effort can learn to "manage" the symptoms and traits; however, their destructive impulses will still be present and the BPD behaviors will still raise their ugly heads like the mythical Hydra. Very few people with BPD are willing to make the effort, or put in the hard work needed, to make any strides in BPD treatment as most lack the insight to even understand how harmful their behaviors are.

We Ozzies need to be realistic and maintain our rational minds when our loved ones are displaying positive behaviors. Just because the person with BPD has behaved themselves for two weeks, that does not mean that they have changed. Remember that they have behavior cycles and that BPD behaviors can be linked directly with stressful periods in their life. The person with BPD may very well have a month where they are a joy to live with. However, once you get too comfortable, or a stressful event pops up in their lives, the BPD behaviors will again arise and be on display. Many Ozzies tend to get overly optimistic during times of improved behavior, only to fall back into depression and confusion when the person with BPD returns to their disordered behavior.

Ozzies that stay in their relationship with the person with BPD must constantly keep in mind that the minimum treatment period for this disorder is 4-10 years of continual intensive therapy. Having expectations of seeing immediate improvements and living happily, just because your loved one agrees to treatment, is unrealistic. If you are a stayer, be prepared for some rough times and enjoy the calm periods. Don't get too comfortable or expect these calm periods to last for extended periods of time. It truly is a matter of enjoying the best and expecting the worst. Remaining realistic about what you expect will pay dividends towards maintaining your own emotional equilibrium.

Be Honest With Yourself: Through the years of living with the person you care about, you have told many lies to other people to protect the person with BPD. You have also told many lies to yourself as a means to justify maintaining the unhealthy relationship. Some of these lies, to yourself, may have been that living with your loved one isn't that bad because, "other people have it worse." Or perhaps, that with your love and support, your loved one will recover from their BPD. The justifications allow you to maintain the relationship just a little longer in hopes that things don't get worse.

In order to complete your journey to Kansas, you have to stop lying to yourself. Stop making comparisons to other Ozzies' situations, and stop telling yourself that you have the power to fix your loved one. Stop thinking the person with BPD will come to a revelation about their condition and suddenly make changes that will allow your relationship to live happily ever after. The hard truth is that it isn't going to happen.

Since you are on your journey to live in reality, you have to be willing to confront it head on. You have to be able to recognize what is true and make a decision to accept it, whether it is positive or negative. Stop trying to make excuses and lies for things that are unacceptable, and call a duck a duck. If you are verbally and emotionally abused, acknowledge it. Don't sugarcoat it or deny it to protect the person engaged in the unacceptable behavior. Lying to yourself to accommodate being harmed is an Oz mentality. Getting your passport to Kansas requires that you be honest with yourself, and others, about what your situation truly is.

A lie that Ozzies will commonly tell is that their situation is "not that bad." They come to this conclusion based on comparing their circumstances with other Ozzies' stories. Everyone's situation is unique, and one Ozzie's ability to tolerate extreme abuse does not justify another's decision to tolerate the abuse they are subjected to. Abuse is abuse, and the decision to tolerate it belittles your self-worth. If you feel you are being mentally, verbally, or physically abused, don't lie to yourself to justify its tolerance. When another Ozzie says they are staying in the relationship because it "isn't that bad", I ask them, "then why did you seek out a support group? Apparently your situation is painful enough that you took the time and effort to seek out other recovering Ozzies in an attempt to cope with the abuse." I will then ask them what they would view as being "too much abuse?" Do they require that the person with BPD be so extreme that they are as unhinged as Joan Crawford in the movie Mommy Dearest?

Staying For The Kids: A common dilemma that arises in the support groups are Ozzies that say they know they should leave. However, they want to keep the family intact because a separation or divorce will be too traumatic on their children. I too fell into this group of Ozzies, as I stayed long after I knew I should have left the marriage, because I was trying to do what was best for my children by maintaining a two-parent home. Of course, every time an Ozzie says this, to themselves or the support group, they follow with, "Well, studies have shown that children grow up more well adjusted and more healthy in a two-parent household." This is only a half-truth.

A two-parent household is better for children, IF the parents have a happy marriage, stable home environment, and are positive role models. A household with a parent with BPD is far from this ideal home environment. There is constant chaos, lack of respect for boundaries, and at a minimum emotional or verbal abuse present. The family members are constantly walking on eggshells around the person with BPD, as both parents display poor examples of coping skills and what a healthy relationship is. As a result of maintaining this unhealthy marriage, the needs of the children to feel safe and secure is thrown out of the window, as the parents are more focused on just maintaining their sanity. A marriage where an abusive parent is present, and there is no safety, is a far different scenario than the ideal two-parent household. It is a much healthier choice, for the children, if the parents separate, are able to provide two stable homes with extended family support, and maintain a safe home environment for the children to grow and mature. Although this is not the ideal family structure, it is healthier than the constant chaos in an abusive marital relationship.

Another substantial concern regarding maintaining the marriage, for the sake of the children, is that BPD can be a learned disorder. By maintaining the marriage while the parent with BPD acts out, the children are observing that borderline responses are normal and appropriate, as well as very effective. As a result, they begin to model the behaviors and engrain them into their personality, passing the traits into the next generation. It is the Ozzie's obligation as the lucid parent to insure that their children have a safe haven to go to, so proper coping behaviors and life skills can be taught. It is important for the children to have at least one parent grounded firmly in Kansas so that they have a chance to be exposed to actual reality where they can mature in a healthy manner.

It is not my intent to suggest that separation or divorce should be an automatic response to finding out that your spouse is diagnosed with BPD. You will likely not find another person that respects marriage more than I do. I would like nothing more than to see all of my fellow Ozzies live happily ever after in their relationships. But, you have to ask yourself if your marriage can be maintained while living up to your other life obligations and duties. Whether one stays or leaves their relationship is a personal choice of each person. In making this decision, what is best for the mental health of the children is something that should be given considerable weight. Variables such as the severity of the displayed BPD traits and how it affects each parents' ability to parent should also be considered.

For Better Or For Worse: A major issue for some Ozzies, particularly those with a strong religious faith, are their wedding vows and promise to love "for better or for worse." After all, if their loved one had been diagnosed with cancer instead of BPD, how could they ever justify abandoning their sick partner? In fact, shouldn't a serious illness be even more reason to say and support their partner in their time of need?

In making the comparison between BPD and other illnesses, one huge factor is often ignored: the abuse the Ozzie suffers at the hands of the person with BPD. Ozzies often justify their staying in the abusive relationship by saying, "if they had cancer, diabetes, or MS, I wouldn't leave. Why is BPD any different?" Quite frankly, because the actions and behaviors that are associated with BPD could place their physical safety and mental health at risk. Conditions associated with cancer, diabetes, or MS, may present great difficulty and require great devotion from a partner, but the conditions do not place the Ozzie's safety at risk. They are conditions that do not result in abusive behavior as an element of their diagnosis. Comparing BPD to these other illnesses is equivalent to comparing apples to oranges.

If you must draw comparisons between illnesses, a more accurate means of measuring is comparing BPD with alcoholism, drug addiction, or spousal abuse. All of these diseases and negative behaviors are destructive to the lives of the person with the condition, as well as the significant other. Would you feel the same loyalty to maintain an abusive relationship if your spouse drank heavily knowing that they became violent while drinking? How about if your spouse was a drug addict that spent all of your money on drugs repeatedly, exposing you to financial hardship and collapse? What if they were offered therapy and rehabilitation, and refused, only to return to a lifestyle that exposed you to hardship and instability? Would you stay and struggle to withstand the storm, or would you take measures to protect yourself? This is the ultimate question you must face in determining whether to maintain or leave your Ozzie/BPD relationship.

The bottom line is, an Ozzie that finds it necessary to leave the relationship does so because of the extreme abuse and instability that they are subjected to. They do not leave simply based on their loved one's diagnosis of a personality disorder. It is important for the Ozzie to understand that a

diagnosis is simply a name given to a cluster of
unhealthy traits. However, if the cluster of traits are
violent and abusive, then the Ozzie is leaving an
abusive and violent relationship, and the name of
the disorder has little relevance. The Ozzie is
addressing their need for safety from the threat of
being harmed and abused.

What about your marriage vows and covenant that
you made to your relationship? How can you
justify breaking this covenant and promise? Take a
second to think about this question. Consider the
abuse in your marriage, and if the vows that were
made to you are being honored.

"I promise to love, honor, and obey, for better or for
worse, in sickness or in health." Where in the vows
does it say that either party has the right to
emotionally, mentally, and physical abuse the other?
Further, where in the vows does it say that either
party has the obligation to subject themselves to
such abuse? Are you fighting to maintain your
vows, while allowing your spouse to trample upon
them time-and-time-again, as they pummel you into
submission, emotionally and/or physically? The
hard truth is that you are likely unconditionally
committed to someone that isn't concerned with
your well-being; which fits nicely into the
codependent section earlier in this book. You are
fighting and sacrificing to maintain an abusive and
unhealthy relationship, one that your partner shows
no regard or intention of honoring.

Chapter 8

Leaving Oz Is A
State Of Mind

Chapter 8

Leaving Oz Is A State Of Mind

As you make your journey towards Kansas you will have to make some decisions what will have a huge impact on yourself, the person with BPD, and your children (if you have children). At the top of this list will be either to remain in the relationship or separate from the person with BPD. This book is not intended to sway your decision one way or the other, as what level of commitment you wish to maintain is your decision, and your decision alone. This book is merely a tool to teach you to take care of yourself, see reality for what it is, and to protect yourself from the various obstacles you will encounter when someone you care about has, or is suspected to have, Borderline Personality Disorder.

There is no cookie cutter answer to tell you to either run for the hills or stay and try to weather the storm. Each relationship is different and circumstances can vary greatly depending upon if there are children being negatively affected, how much abuse is present, if the person with BPD is truly making an effort to address their disorder, the severity of the BPD behaviors, and last but not least, what your boundaries are.

Completing your trip to Kansas is not about physical distance from the person with BPD. It is not about dealing with the person with BPD or trying to understand all of their behaviors and reasons for those behaviors. Completing your trip to Kansas is about YOU, the Ozzie. Your journey actually has very little to do with the person with BPD in your life. Arriving in Kansas is about understanding yourself, what led to your relationship with someone that has BPD traits, what you received emotionally from the unhealthy relationship, and how to change aspects about yourself that allowed the abuse to continue for so long. It is about teaching yourself to not tolerate abuse, why you tolerated it, and that you are worth more than being an emotional punching bag for someone that feels poorly about themselves. Whether you can make the needed changes while maintaining your relationship with this person is completely up to you to determine.

Plain and simple, Kansas/reality is a state of mind. It is a state of mind that you, the Ozzie, needs to achieve to stay mentally healthy. It is about living in the same world that other mentally healthy people live in, and recognizing when the person with BPD is trying to project their warped illusions onto you. It is about knowing that it is healthy to have interpersonal relationships with friends and family, and to participate in everyday activities that you enjoy. It is about knowing who you are as a person, and not having to constantly sacrifice yourself for the benefit of another as they drain your emotional gas tank and leave you on empty. It is about owning your own emotions and feelings, and being allowed to be happy without being forced to take on the burden of someone else's misery. Kansas is about the Ozzie's journey, not about the person with BPD.

Escaping Oz requires more than the Ozzie merely ending the relationship or creating physical distance between them and their abuser. In some situations that may be warranted and very necessary. But keep in mind that an Ozzie can leave an Ozzie/BPD relationship, and think this alone allows them to escape all their worries. They can move far away, start a new life, and assume that they have left their unhealthy partnership in their rearview mirror, while blaming the person with BPD for the failure of the relationship. However, as they begin to start new relationships, they notice a pattern of the partner they choose and see that these new relationships may be every bit as destructive as the one they attempted to escape. While the Ozzie continued to blame the person with BPD for the failed relationship, they failed to leave Oz because they did not address their own unhealthy beliefs, and traits, that played a part in the codependent relationship dynamic. The Ozzie just found a new relationship in which those unhealthy traits could exist again. Making it to Kansas is not about the Ozzie's geography or their partner. It's about understanding themselves and making the necessary changes to maintain healthy relationships.

On the other side of the coin there are Ozzies that decide to stay and maintain their relationship with the person with BPD. Some of these Ozzies have happy, productive lives, and have strong enough boundaries that they can properly cope with living with a partner with BPD. As individuals they know who they are, know where they are going, and can detach from their loved one's disorder enough to maintain their own sanity and mental health. Does this make their loved one any less BPD? No, but it definitely influences how much the person with BPD can disrupt the Ozzie's life. As Ozzies, our priority is taking care of our own lives, emotions, and needs, and not allowing the person with BPD to control them.

On my journey I found it necessary to leave my marriage due to the truly destructive behavior my wife displayed, as well as my inability to get myself healthy while maintaining that relationship. The dangerous behaviors she attempted to utilize could have easily resulted in my incarceration as a result of her false allegations. When her behavior escalated to the extreme of being dangerous, I had to make a choice between taking care of myself, my future, and my children's future, or play a game of Russian Roulette with our lives. Leaving, in my case, was more about protecting my safety and security, and having an inability to protect myself while being physically in the same household. However, after I left, I still had to do the homework on myself, and address my own destructive personality traits to complete my journey. It is important for Ozzies to understand that physical space does not signify escaping Oz. Nor does staying in the relationship with a person with BPD keep you in Oz. You decide through your actions, beliefs, perceptions of reality, boundaries, and love for yourself, where you reside. You have the power and control to decide if you take up residency in Oz or Kansas. Which will you choose?

AFTERWARDS

Ozzie Tinman
20 Years Later

Afterwards
Ozzie Tinman 20 Years Later

This year One Way Ticket To Kansas celebrated its 20 Year Anniversary. Over this time, I have had the honor of interacting with numerous Ozzies as they shared their story, requested advice, and made their transition to Kansas. I have witnessed both, success stories as well as Ozzies that fell short of their goals. I have personally met with Ozzies from as far away as England, as well as some that live right in my own city in Southern California. Each one shared their story of overcoming their fears and reclaiming their lives. I was touched by each person that chose to personally contact me and trust me with their stories.

I am humbled and proud that what began as a project that was meant to be distributed to a handful of support group members, has led to a book that has sold approximately 20,000 copies. It brings me peace that my experience with my ex-wife, diagnosed with BPD, was not in vain, as it has allowed me to extend a helping hand to thousands of Ozzies as they struggle with similar experiences. This situation has also allowed me to share my experiences at the annual conference for the National Alliance on Mental Illness (NAMI), where I have served multiple times as a guest speaker. As part of this experience, I was able to give first-hand accounts to mental health professionals regarding the impact this disorder has on the families of someone diagnosed with BPD. As I spoke to these professionals, it was rewarding to observe that the mental health community recognizes the need for treatment for those who have someone diagnosed with BPD in their lives. It is wonderful to see the exponential strides that are made every year.

In my interactions with Ozzies over the last 20 years, one of the questions I am always asked is where my life has taken me since One Way Ticket To Kansas was published in 2005. So, for the 20 Year Anniversary of my book, I would like to share my life experiences, while in Kansas, from 2005-2025.

I am happy to report that after divorcing my ex-wife in 2005, I never returned to Oz, and remained firmly in Kansas. Of course, life had its hurdles since I did have two children with my ex, so there was still co-parenting and interactions that we would have in the raising of our children. However, understanding the manipulation tactics that she would attempt to utilize, I insisted that all interaction with her was business-like and contact was only when absolutely necessary for the children. My ex-wife attempted to utilize any tools she could to interfere with my life moving forward, including the court system, the children, and engaging in regular distortion campaigns. What I learned quickly was if I refused to engage with her and remained on the high road, it muted almost all of her attacks. Despite her attempts to initiate conflict, she would quickly exhaust herself and give up if I refused to throw fuel on the fire.

In regards to court, she would attempt to utilize child custody and child support as a reason to bring matters before a judge as a means of having the judge order strict terms and conditions of our shared custody agreement. Anything she interpreted as not strictly adhering to the Court's orders, she immediately scheduled a hearing to accuse me of violating the Court's orders. Although this tactic was somewhat effective in the beginning, the Court quickly recognized that I was compliant with its orders as I made it a point to continually focus on wanting to do what was best for the children and their growth. It didn't take long for the Court to recognize that her regularly scheduled court hearings were nothing but a control tactic in which she would attempt to utilize the might of the Court for her advantage. As the Court noticed this trend, and as I maintained the high road of only focusing on the best interests of the children, the rulings began to favor me at every turn. Eventually the Court expressed its dissatisfaction with her manipulations and even her attorney "fired her" as a client due her being proven to be lying during a court proceeding. Without the use of the court system, and my refusal to interact with her, my ex-wife eventually had no choice but to seek conflict and chaos elsewhere.

Despite her focusing most of her attention elsewhere, the distortion campaigns continued for years. Periodically I would come across mutual friends that would inform me about the things she was saying, but I would simply tell them that I wasn't interested. Some people believed her, and some people didn't, and I wasn't going to waste my time getting sucked back into a game of he said-she said. After all, that was exactly the response she would want. I also found that allowing people to witness and judge things for themselves was very effective, as in time her lies always came to light. As people discovered that they were manipulated and deceived, they quickly cut ties with her. Although allowing this process to unfold took time, in the end karma always put the universe back in balance and she paid the consequences by losing people that once supported her.

Following my divorce I focused primary on raising my children and rebuilding bridges at my job. The stress and chaos of the ending of my marriage took its toll on my ability to focus at work, and I knew building back the trust of people I worked with would be a long road. For my children, I focused on creating a stable and loving environment during the 50% of the time that they were with me. I knew that they would have an uphill climb as they grew since they would still be exposed to the chaos of having a mother with BPD, but I understood that I did not have any control over that. I only had control over the time that they were with me, and my goal was for them to maintain their footing in Kansas as I attempted to keep them grounded in reality. I maintained the belief that given the choice between a stable and loving environment vs a chaotic and unstable environment, they would choose to develop healthy traits and coping strategies. During this period of time, the treatment for BPD was a relatively new field, and the treatment for family members was almost non-existent. Much of raising my children, while attempting to keep them grounded in reality, was trial and error. I also refused to engage in criticizing their mother or even telling them that she had a personality disorder. When they would come to me and share some of the odd or negative behaviors their mother exhibited, I would talk to them, ask them how it made them feel, and ask them how they would have handled things differently if they were her. Their answers always surprised me in regards to how much they understood and how mature their solutions were. I took the stance that as long as they recognized that their mother's coping mechanisms were not productive or positive, then they were maintaining at least one foot in Kansas.

As my children grew they both excelled in their own way. My son was very social, somewhat popular in school, and played sports. He loved working with his hands, and from a young age expressed that he wanted to be a mechanic. I remember when he was two years old, he would line up his Hot Wheels cars and have a "car show", walking his fingers through the lines of cars as if it were a person observing the cars. As he grew, he continued his interest in cars and when it was time for him to drive, he found his first car, a 1964 Barracuda, sitting inoperable in someone's backyard. We made the owner an offer on the car and towed it home. Within weeks he had gone through the engine, made repairs, and got it running. I was surprised as the seller had told us the car hadn't ran in years, as it just sat in the backyard following the death of his father. My son had repaired it within a matter of weeks and proudly drove it to school daily. He continued his love for cars by going to mechanics trade school and getting his certification. As he grew and matured, he did not allow the chaos within his childhood to affect the development of him doing what he loved. He understood that his mother experienced difficulty with processing the world and reality, yet he maintained respect for her, and learned to navigate around the pitfalls that she would attempt to lay for him to fall into. He remained grounded in Kansas, and although he loves his mother, he also understands that maintaining healthy boundaries with her is a necessity for him to have his own life. At the age of 28, he has navigated the waters of having a mother with BPD like a true captain of a ship.

Throughout her school years my daughter excelled at academics and participated in theater. She was the type of student that grasped onto knowledge quickly, and easily achieved straight A's despite not having to study much. She loved acting and participating in theater productions, and earned a few main roles on stage. She also took a large interest in music, and going to concerts together was one of the avenues in which we bonded as a father and daughter. I liked to call her my "punk rock girl" because she had a rebellious spirit and she greatly enjoyed the punk rock and metalcore music scene, where people of all walks of life were accepted and concerts were small and very fan oriented. In regards to her relationship with her mother, the closeness that she a I had did result in some difficulty for her. As her mother knew that we were very close as a father and daughter, this led to period where me ex would split our daughter black, finding fault in virtually everything she did. She chastised her dress attire, her music, who she was as a person, and eventually started to begin projecting onto my daughter and accusing her of being mentally ill. This eventually led to my ex taking our daughter to a psychologist who prescribed her unneeded medications. I attempted to take the matter to court to cease the medications, but the Court ruled that if a doctor had prescribed the medications then I had to allow and support it. This mis-prescribing of medications began a downward spiral for my daughter as her body attempted to adjust to foreign chemicals that were altering her behavior when they weren't really needed. Although it didn't drastically affect her high school academic performance, it would later impact her ability to transition into a college environment as the medications had a sedative effect on her, making it difficult to focus. Despite the medication hurdles, and the negative relationship she had with her mother, my daughter continued to push forward, attempting to find her path in this world to do something she loved. This path took her from a large college in California to a small community college in Oregon, and learning many life lessons along the way regarding family, friendships and finding contentment. She eventually returned to California where she made the decision to address her medication situation, and begin to get a grasp on the what she was prescribed and whether the medications were truly needed. She began to ween herself off various unneeded medications, with the help of a therapist, and took control of herself as an adult. She was eventually able to find equilibrium and regained the ability to function without the impact of medications that only served to sedate and cloud her thought process. After regaining her clarity, she settled on pursuing a career in Forensic Sciences, where she could utilize her life experiences of dealing with a mentally ill mother as well as my background in law enforcement. She decided that she wanted to give back to the mental health community as well as work in law enforcement to reflect the roads that she had traveled during her first 24 years of life. She re-enrolled back in college where she has been continuing her studies in Psychology for the last year and a half. She is excelling with straight A's and finding that she has again found her element in academics.

I am proud of my daughter for overcoming the struggles and obstacles that her mother placed in her path that included sabotage, emotional attacks, and creating self-doubt in her. Not to mention, creating a situation that involved overmedication and my daughter having to come to an awareness that the prescriptions that were supposed to be helping her function were achieving just the opposite. My daughter's journey required her to trust and believe in herself, and despite the negativity and attacks designed to break her down, she raised up and became a stronger person that is now thriving. My daughter continues to struggle with her relationship with her mother, as her mother continues to alternate between splitting her black and white. But through this experience she has learned the ques and warnings that are in her mother's behavior that allow her to predict when a behavior change may be on the horizon. She continues to attempt to have a relationship with her mother, while still maintaining boundaries and maintaining her self-respect.

As mentioned earlier in this update, one of the major ways in which escaping Oz affected my life after my marriage was in my employment. During the time that I was confronting my ex-wife's false allegations and dealing with the years of abuse that she directed at me, my work performance suffered greatly. I went through a period of deep depression and was not motivated to continue excelling in my work environment. Prior to my world coming to a crash-landing, I was considered an officer with great potential of rising up the ranks, and had received many awards and recognitions. When my work performance began to be impacted, it resulted in my superiors noticing the decline and my prospects for advances were affected. In addition to this, my ex-wife had a mutual friend with our Chief, and she utilized this connection to spread the rumor to my Chief that I abused my wife and was polygraphed for molesting my children. As you can imagine, the optics of promoting someone with these allegations became a scarlet letter that followed me for years, and made me unpromotable. As time passed, my superiors forgot about the allegations, and people wondered why I was not being promoted. Unfortunately, it was already established that I was someone that got over-looked, repeatedly, for advancement and that is a difficult barrier to overcome. I accepted that I didn't have any control over this situation or the bias that our Chief had developed against me. As such, I focused on being the best Corporal in our department. If that meant that I stalled at the rank of Corporal, then so be it, but at least I would rebuild my reputation as an officer that Sergeants would fight over to have as their backup. Year after year I proved to my superiors that I was an officer that deserved their trust and found fulfillment in doing a good job. The status of having an extra bar on my shirt became irrelevant to me as I knew I didn't need another shiny lapel pin to let others know that I had value to my department. My hard work resulted in my having an open invitation to pick my assignments and work under any Sergeant that I chose. It gave me the flexibility to work in assignments that I enjoyed, rather than being told where I had to work, as well as having the ability to pick my schedule. I saw the silver lining in the situation, as very few officers in our department enjoyed the independence that I was entrusted with, and enjoyed. I may not have had another bar on my shirt, but I had the respect and trust of everyone that I worked with. I had fulfillment knowing that the work I was doing mattered and that those I worked closely with had complete trust in my abilities. When my work life found balance, I found appreciation that did not require a title or chevron to signify my value.

In July of 2013 I met the woman that I would entrust to become my future wife. We met online through a dating website, and with that comes a certain level of skepticism and guardedness. We had agreed to meet at a public location, then drive together to the Pageant of the Master in Laguna Beach for our first date. Upon meeting her in person, her first question to me was, "you aren't going to kill me are you?" I assured her that I had forgotten my shovel and tarp, so I would have to wait until our next date to complete that dastardly plan. She laughed, and I was happy to see that she had a sense of humor that was compatible with that of a law enforcement officer. The date went well, and we began to see each other regularly. Over our 2 years of dating, I learned that she too had experienced a difficult prior marriage, and had been exposed to unacceptable treatment by a spouse. She was open about her past, was kind, loving, and accepting of the trials that my children and I had been though. She was someone that made no judgements, and trusted the truthfulness of the experiences that I shared with her. It was refreshing to be trusted when talking about my past, as most people respond, "Another crazy ex story huh? Everyone has a crazy ex." For someone that has been through the experience of dealing with ex with BPD, the abuse being minimized can be like hearing nails on a chalkboard. The dating process and the growth of the relationship went very smoothly as we were both people that were appreciative of finding a stable partner that reciprocated the love and trust we gave one another. We married in November of 2015 and have enjoyed a happy marriage for over nine years. I have found that having a healthy and loving relationship, where both partners' emotional gas tanks are filled, is highly rewarding and something that serves as the foundation of waking up every morning thankful and appreciative of the person laying next to me.

Long gone are the days of being belittled and chastised over minor mistakes. Long gone are the nightly marathons of rage behavior as you are told how evil you are and how you deserve the abuse being hurled in your direction. Long gone are the delusional accusations, the intentional attempts to harm you, and the belief that you aren't deserving of self-respect and kindness. After you find a partner that shares genuine love, acceptance, kindness, and values you, all the hurt of the past dissipates into nothingness, until one day you wake up and all you feel is love and happiness.

I am thankful for the exponential happiness that my wife has brought into my life. At the age of 52, we are now planning the next stage of our life, as well as when we will exit our respective professional careers for the greener pastures of retirement. Will be end up in Florida, or Texas, or Georgia, or perhaps actually physically in Kansas? At the current moment, we are enjoying making these decision together, and weighing the options that offer the best benefits for a retired couple. It is a wonderful gift to have a loving partner that you can plan a future with; one that considers your opinions, wants and needs, as much as they do their own. Regardless of where we do decide to reside in retirement, we will be there together, enjoying the love and support of a healthy relationship. A relationship where I can walk in the front door and say to myself, "There's no place like home."

Appendix

Ozzie Dictionary

Appendix

Ozzie Dictionary

When communicating with other Ozzies or reading literature about Borderline Personality Disorder, you will come across terms that have specific meanings to the Ozzie Community. Some of these terms are initials, acronyms, and clinical labels. Other terms may be actual words, but have slightly different meanings within the community. Below are some of the common terms used, and their meanings, in the Ozzie communities. Keep in mind that dialog in the communities is ever growing and changing. As you come across new terms, make notes so you can refer back to them when needed.

Abandonment: The fear of a person with BPD that the Ozzie will eventually leave. This can be imagined or real, but is a constant fear of someone with BPD.

Acting Out: A defense mechanism when a person displays behaviors and actions to express an emotion that is being experienced. Acting out could range from huge displays of anger to engaging in self-harm.

Apple Trees: A metaphor taken from the Wizard of Oz, in which Dorothy picking an apple resulted in her being attacked by the apple trees. This metaphor refers to the personal attacks the person with BPD engages in against the Ozzie for everyday behaviors that do not justify an attack.

Boundaries: The parameters that a person sets that indicate what behaviors that person will and will not tolerate being directed towards them. Boundaries can set physical and emotional limits.

BPD: Initials for Borderline Personality Disorder. The initials can also refer to a person that has actually been diagnosed with Borderline Personality Disorder by a qualified clinician. However, note that some people consider it insensitive to call someone "the BPD" as it can be interpreted as defining the person as the disorder. When this book was initially written it was acceptable, and there may still be active members that use the term rather than saying, "the person with BPD."

Catch 22: A situation that a person with BPD creates so that the Ozzie is presented in a negative light regardless of what action they take. This usually occurs while the person with BPD is in the process of splitting the Ozzie "black" to validate the belief that the Ozzie is a bad person.

Codependency: Repeatedly sacrificing oneself on behalf of another, as a means of maintaining an unhealthy relationship. This could involve a situation where one party continually gives without any reciprocation. This will often lead to resentment, and feelings of being taken advantage of.

Crazy-Making: A term used to describe the irrational behaviors, beliefs, and manipulations by a person with BPD that results in the Ozzie feeling like they are being driven crazy.

Defense Mechanism: A subconscious response intended to protect a person from establishing a negative self-image and minimize anxiety.

Denial: A defense mechanism where a person fails to recognize obvious implications or consequences of an act or situation. Denial can also indicate a person that is unable to recognize his or her own obvious negative or harmful behaviors.

Dissociation: A defense mechanism in which a person's actions are no longer a response to the current situation and circumstances before them. In regards to BPD, their responses are often reflecting their pain and trauma from their past or childhood.

Distortion Campaign: When a person with BPD deliberately tries to convince family, friends, and other important people in your life, that you are the person that is "sick", abusive, lies, is violent, and can involve false allegations of criminal behavior. This is an extreme response to discredit the Ozzie, and for the person with BPD to receive sympathy for portraying themselves as the victim.

Dorothy: A metaphor for an Ozzie that is confused, searching for logic, finds that they have lost touch with reality, and is emotionally lost. Dorothy represents an Ozzie that is just trying to make sense of the skewed reality they find themselves in.

False Hope: An Ozzie's over optimistic and unrealistic belief that the person with BPD will suddenly get better and realize their destructive behaviors.

Fix: The Ozzie's false belief that they have the ability to save the person with BPD from their disorder by curing their disorder, providing them knowledge, or interjecting in the person's treatment.

Fixation: An Ozzie that submerges themselves in seeking information about BPD so much that it begins to negatively impact other important aspect of their life.

Fleas: When an Ozzie adopts destructive traits from the person with BPD. This happens when the Ozzie begins to believe that the borderline responses are "normal."

Hoover: The process in which a person with BPD will suck the Ozzie back into an unhealthy relationship. The person with BPD will often do this with kindness when they sense they are about to be abandoned. They may also Hoover through the use of fear (distortion campaigns, false allegations, etc.).

Horse Of A Different Color: A metaphor from the Wizard of Oz, which represents the ever changing world of the Ozzie. The horse in the movie constantly changes colors with every scene, as does the world and reality of the Ozzie.

Isolation: The process in which a person with BPD completely cuts the Ozzie off from friend, family and outside sources of emotional support. It is a control tactic to keep the Ozzie dependent on the person with BPD, and from leaving the relationship.

Kansan: A person that lives in a mentally healthy and stable reality.

Kansas: A metaphor for a reality that is consistent with a person that is mentally healthy. A reality where rules are consistent, based in logic, and well defined.

Light Bulb Effect: When an Ozzie has a moment of clarity in which they realize their perceptions are skewed, and they recognize reality. The Ozzie also realizes that they are not alone in their struggles and feel connected with other Ozzies.

Lion: A metaphor for having courage and facing adversity.

Mirroring: A person with BPD has an uncanny ability to mimic or "mirror" the actions, beliefs, or values of those around them to give the impression of connectedness and belonging. It is a tactic to assimilate into a group without their flaw of lacking an identity being detected.

NPD: Narcissistic Personality Disorder. Many Ozzies find that the person with BPD is very self centered, lacks empathy for other people, and has little regard for anyone other than themselves. As a result, some people diagnosed with BPD will also be given a dual-diagnosis of NPD.

Non: A person that cares about someone that has been diagnosed with BPD. It is the counterpart of referring to the person with BPD as "the BPD" (i.e., "the Non"). This term originated from the book, Stop Walking On Eggshells. It has been universally adopted in treatment circles to refer to the person that has a relationship with a mentally ill or addicted person.

Oz: A skewed reality full of distortion and lies. It is the "reality" that is created by the person with BPD, and is purely based on that person's emotions and perceptions. It is void of logic, rationale, consistency, or defined rules. It is ever changing.

Ozzie: A person that is not diagnosed with BPD, that cares about someone that has been diagnosed or suspected to have BPD. In some support communities an Ozzie can graduate to a Kansan when they are able to develop a healthy sense of reality.

Paranoia: A person's irrational belief that someone, or something, is trying to cause harm to them or someone they care about.

Pedestal: When the person with BPD deifies or has an overly exaggerated, undeserved, sense of adoration for the Ozzie. This occurred when the Ozzie is split white.

Projection: A defense mechanism where the person attributes their emotions and feeling onto another person. A person with BPD will project their negative emotions and feelings onto the Ozzie so they (person with BPD) does not have to take responsibility for them.

Projection Identification: When an Ozzie accepts a projected feeling or emotion as their own, and identifies with them.

Scarecrow: A metaphor indicating the Ozzie's quest to logically determine reality (Kansas) from illusion (Oz). It also indicates the Ozzie educating themselves about BPD and how it affects them.

Self-Blaming: An Ozzie that unjustly blames themselves for the actions, behaviors, beliefs, or the mental condition of the person with BPD.

Self-Fulfilling Prophecy: When a person with BPD makes a prediction of a future event, then intentionally creates a situation where the predicted outcome is likely to result. They fulfill their own prophecy.

Splitting: A defense mechanism where a person with BPD sees someone they have a relationship with as "all good" (white) or "all bad" (black). Splitting is the process in which the person with BPD goes from one extreme view to another, alternating between good and evil. A person with BPD has a very limited ability to see "the gray area" of people or situations.

Strength Reminders/Mementos: A physical object that serves as a reminder for the Ozzie of what their goals and motivations are during their journey to Kansas. The item usually carries a significant personal meaning to the Ozzie.

Stinkin' Thinkin': When an Ozzie begins to have unhealthy, irrational, or distorted thoughts that will have a negative impact on their journey to Kansas. Such thinking often results in being hoovered back into living in a distorted reality. This is also referred to as Oz Thinking or Non-Sense.

SWOE: The initials for the book: Stop Walking On Eggshells, written by Paul T Mason and Randi Kreger. This is one of the most influential books in the Ozzie/Non communities.

Tin Man: A metaphor for an Ozzie that needs to find love and care for themselves. The Tin Man reflects the belief that one must find love for themselves before they are able to share love with another in a healthy manner.

Tornado: A metaphor for the whirlwind of emotions and chaos felt by the Ozzie while they are involved in the BPD relationship.

Wizard: A metaphor for the person with BPD and the illusion that they create for their persona. The person with BPD projects an image of greatness. However, when their true self is revealed they are nothing more than a scared person afraid of the world around them. Their life is an illusion, hidden behind a well draped façade.